Publisher 2010: Basic

Student Manual

Publisher 2010: Basic

President, Axzo Press:	Jon Winder
Vice President, Product Development:	Charles G. Blum
Vice President, Operations:	Josh Pincus
Director of Publishing Systems Development:	Dan Quackenbush
Writer:	Chris Hale
Copyeditor:	Cathy Albano
Keytester:	Cliff Coryea

Trademarks

ILT Series is a trademark of Axzo Press.

Some of the product names and company names used in this book have been used for identification purposes only and may be trademarks or registered trademarks of their respective manufacturers and sellers.

Disclaimer

We reserve the right to revise this publication and make changes from time to time in its content without notice.

Student Manual
ISBN 10: 1-4260-2060-0
ISBN 13: 978-1-4260-2060-5

Student Manual with Disc
ISBN-10: 1-4260-2062-7
ISBN-13: 978-1-4260-2062-9

Printed in the United States of America

2 3 4 5 6 7 GL 14 13 12 11

Contents

Introduction

After reading this introduction, you will know how to:

A Use ILT Series manuals in general.

B Use prerequisites, a target student description, course objectives, and a skills inventory to properly set your expectations for the course.

C Re-key this course after class.

Topic A: About the manual

ILT Series philosophy

Our manuals facilitate your learning by providing structured interaction with the software itself. While we provide text to explain difficult concepts, the hands-on activities are the focus of our courses. By paying close attention as your instructor leads you through these activities, you will learn the skills and concepts effectively.

We believe strongly in the instructor-led class. During class, focus on your instructor. Our manuals are designed and written to facilitate your interaction with your instructor, and not to call attention to manuals themselves.

We believe in the basic approach of setting expectations, delivering instruction, and providing summary and review afterwards. For this reason, lessons begin with objectives and end with summaries. We also provide overall course objectives and a course summary to provide both an introduction to and closure on the entire course.

Manual components

The manuals contain these major components:

- Table of contents
- Introduction
- Units
- Course summary
- Glossary
- Index

Each element is described below.

Table of contents

The table of contents acts as a learning roadmap.

Introduction

The introduction contains information about our training philosophy and our manual components, features, and conventions. It contains target student, prerequisite, objective, and setup information for the specific course.

Units

Units are the largest structural component of the course content. A unit begins with a title page that lists objectives for each major subdivision, or topic, within the unit. Within each topic, conceptual and explanatory information alternates with hands-on activities. Units conclude with a summary comprising one paragraph for each topic, and an independent practice activity that gives you an opportunity to practice the skills you've learned.

The conceptual information takes the form of text paragraphs, exhibits, lists, and tables. The activities are structured in two columns, one telling you what to do, the other providing explanations, descriptions, and graphics.

Course summary

This section provides a text summary of the entire course. It is useful for providing closure at the end of the course. The course summary also indicates the next course in this series, if there is one, and lists additional resources you might find useful as you continue to learn about the software.

Glossary

The glossary provides definitions for all of the key terms used in this course.

Index

The index at the end of this manual makes it easy for you to find information about a particular software component, feature, or concept.

Manual conventions

We've tried to keep the number of elements and the types of formatting to a minimum in the manuals. This aids in clarity and makes the manuals more classically elegant looking. But there are some conventions and icons you should know about.

Item	Description
Italic text	In conceptual text, indicates a new term or feature.
Bold text	In unit summaries, indicates a key term or concept. In an independent practice activity, indicates an explicit item that you select, choose, or type.
`Code font`	Indicates code or syntax.
`Longer strings of ▶ code will look ▶ like this.`	In the hands-on activities, any code that's too long to fit on a single line is divided into segments by one or more continuation characters (▶). This code should be entered as a continuous string of text.
Select **bold item**	In the left column of hands-on activities, bold sans-serif text indicates an explicit item that you select, choose, or type.
Keycaps like ⏎ ENTER	Indicate a key on the keyboard you must press.

Hands-on activities

The hands-on activities are the most important parts of our manuals. They are divided into two primary columns. The "Here's how" column gives short instructions to you about what to do. The "Here's why" column provides explanations, graphics, and clarifications. Here's a sample:

Do it!

A-1:   Creating a commission formula

Here's how	Here's why
1 Open Sales	This is an oversimplified sales compensation worksheet. It shows sales totals, commissions, and incentives for five sales reps.
2 Observe the contents of cell F4	F4 ▼ = =E4*C_Rate The commission rate formulas use the name "C_Rate" instead of a value for the commission rate.

For these activities, we have provided a collection of data files designed to help you learn each skill in a real-world business context. As you work through the activities, you will modify and update these files. Of course, you might make a mistake and therefore want to re-key the activity starting from scratch. To make it easy to start over, you will rename each data file at the end of the first activity in which the file is modified. Our convention for renaming files is to add the word "My" to the beginning of the file name. In the above activity, for example, a file called "Sales" is being used for the first time. At the end of this activity, you would save the file as "My sales," thus leaving the "Sales" file unchanged. If you make a mistake, you can start over using the original "Sales" file.

In some activities, however, it might not be practical to rename the data file. If you want to retry one of these activities, ask your instructor for a fresh copy of the original data file.

Topic B: Setting your expectations

Properly setting your expectations is essential to your success. This topic will help you do that by providing:

- Prerequisites for this course
- A description of the target student
- A list of the objectives for the course
- A skills assessment for the course

Course prerequisites

Before taking this course, you should be familiar with personal computers and the use of a keyboard and a mouse. Furthermore, this course assumes that you've completed the following course or have equivalent experience:

- *Windows 7: Basic*

Target student

Students will benefit from this course if your goal is to learn the basic features of Publisher 2010 to create both basic and multi-page publications, work with master pages, format text and paragraphs, work with tables, and create publications for sharing and commercial printing.

Course objectives

These overall course objectives will give you an idea about what to expect from the course. It is also possible that they will help you see that this course is not the right one for you. If you think you either lack the prerequisite knowledge or already know most of the subject matter to be covered, you should let your instructor know that you think you are misplaced in the class.

After completing this course, you will know how to:

- Identify components of the Publisher 2010 interface, open a publication, use Backstage view, navigate a publication and change the zoom level, select text, and get help using Publisher.
- Create a new publication, add basic elements to a layout, and position elements precisely using guides and the Measurement task pane.
- Create a facing-pages layout, insert pages, move items between publications, and work with master pages.
- Link and unlink text boxes, add continuation notices, set tab stops, format paragraphs, control indents and spacing, and create drop caps.
- Create tables and create a table from imported data, modify a table's structure, format tables, and edit an Excel spreadsheet in Publisher.
- Position text in text boxes, apply text box styles and effects, add columns to text boxes, adjust text wrap, modify pictures, adjust stacking order, and group items.
- Print publications, export publications to PDF format, check spelling, apply design checks, and prepare a publication for commercial printing.

Skills inventory

Use the following form to gauge your skill level entering the class. For each skill listed, rate your familiarity from 1 to 5, with 5 being the most familiar. *This is not a test.* Rather, it is intended to provide you with an idea of where you're starting from at the beginning of class. If you're wholly unfamiliar with all the skills, you might not be ready for the class. If you think you already understand all of the skills, you might need to move on to the next course in the series. In either case, you should let your instructor know as soon as possible.

Skill	1	2	3	4	5
Identifying and using interface components					
Adding a command to the Quick Access toolbar					
Viewing and editing publication properties					
Navigating pages and zooming					
Using the mouse to select text					
Using Publisher Help					
Creating a new publication					
Creating and inserting text in a publication					
Inserting pictures into a publication					
Defining a custom color					
Positioning objects					
Aligning and distributing objects					
Inserting pages in a publication					
Editing the default master page					
Creating and applying master pages					
Linking and unlinking text boxes					
Adding continuation notices					
Setting tab stops and leaders					
Creating indents					
Creating a bulleted list					
Applying a keep setting					
Adjusting vertical spacing					

Skill	1	2	3	4	5
Creating a drop cap					
Creating a table					
Importing and modifying an Excel document					
Modifying table cells					
Applying table formats					
Shading table cells					
Aligning text within table cells					
Formatting cell borders					
Inserting graphics into table cells					
Positioning text within a text box					
Fitting text to a text box					
Applying styles to a text box					
Changing text box columns					
Controlling text wrap					
Adjusting picture brightness					
Applying picture styles					
Recoloring a picture					
Grouping objects					
Stacking objects					
Printing a publication					
Saving a publication as a PDF document					
Checking spelling					
Checking a design for errors					
Preparing a publication for commercial printing					

Topic C: Re-keying the course

If you have the proper hardware and software, you can re-key this course after class. This section explains what you'll need in order to do so, and how to do it.

Hardware requirements

Your personal computer should have:

- A keyboard and a mouse
- A 500 MHz (or faster) processor
- At least 256 MB of available RAM
- At least 1.5 GB of available hard drive
- A monitor with at least 1,024 × 768 resolution

Software requirements

You will also need the following software:

- Microsoft Windows 7 (You can also use Windows Vista or Windows XP, although the screen shots in this course were taken using Windows 7, so your screens might look somewhat different.)
- Microsoft Publisher 2010
- Microsoft Excel 2010
- Adobe Reader
- A printer driver (An actual printer is not required, but students will not be able to complete Activity A-1 in the unit titled "Finalizing publications" unless a driver is installed.)

Network requirements

The following network components and connectivity are also required for rekeying this course:

- Internet access, for the following purposes:
  - Downloading the latest critical updates and service packs
  - Opening Help files at Microsoft Office Online (If online Help is not available, students will not be able to complete Activity C-1 in the unit titled "Getting started.")
  - Downloading the student data files from www.axzopress.com (if necessary)

Setup instructions to re-key the course

Before you re-key the course, you will need to perform the following steps.

1 Use Windows Update to install all available critical updates and Service Packs.

2 If using a flat panel display, we recommend using the panel's native resolution for best results. Color depth/quality should be set to High (24 bit) or higher.

Please note that your display settings or resolution may differ from the author's, and so your screens might not exactly match the screen shots in this manual.

3 If necessary, reset any Microsoft Publisher 2010 defaults that you have changed. If you do not wish to reset the defaults, you can still re-key the course, but some activities might not work exactly as documented.

a On the Quick Access toolbar, right-click commands other than Save, Undo, and Redo and choose Remove from Quick Access Toolbar.

b Remove words added to the custom dictionary. (On the File tab, click Options; in the Proofing category, click Custom Dictionaries; then click Edit Word List. In the CUSTOM.DIC dialog box, click Delete all.)

4 If you have the data disc that came with this manual, locate the Student Data folder on it and copy it to the desktop of your computer.

If you don't have the data disc, you can download the Student Data files for the course:

a Connect to www.axzopress.com.

b Under Downloads, click Instructor-Led Training.

c Browse the subject categories to locate your course. Then click the course title to display a list of available downloads. (You can also access these downloads through our Catalog listings.)

d Click the link(s) for downloading the student data files.

e Create a folder named Student Data on the desktop of your computer.

f Double-click the downloaded zip file(s) and drag the contents into the Student Data folder.

Unit 1

Getting started

Unit time: 60 minutes

Complete this unit, and you'll know how to:

A Start Publisher, identify components of the Publisher 2010 interface, open an existing publication, and use Backstage view.

B Navigate, change the zoom level, and select text in a publication.

C Get help using Publisher 2010.

Topic A: The Publisher interface

Explanation

Publisher 2010 is a desktop publishing program that you can use to create a variety of different publications, such as newsletters, brochures, and business documents. Although word processing programs such as Microsoft Word provide features for working with text and graphics, they don't offer the same degree of control over layout and design that a desktop publishing program does.

Starting Publisher

To start Publisher, click the Start button and choose All Programs, Microsoft Office, Microsoft Publisher 2010. The New section of the File tab appears; from here, you can select the type of publication you want to create. Publisher offers templates for brochures, business cards, newsletters, and other types of publications. By using a template, you can start with a design and then add your own text and images. You can also start from scratch with a blank publication.

Opening publications

To open a previously saved publication, click the File tab and then click Open. You can also press Ctrl+O if you're viewing another tab. If you already have one publication open and you want to open another, the second publication appears in a separate window. To switch between the two windows, you can use the View tab, the taskbar buttons, or press Alt+Tab.

To open an existing publication:

1   Click the File tab.
2   Click Open. The Open Publication dialog box appears.
3   Navigate to the folder that contains the publication you want to open.
4   Select the publication that you want to open.
5   Click Open.

Do it!

A-1: Opening an existing publication

The files for this activity are in Student Data folder **Unit 1\Topic A**.

Here's how	Here's why
1 Click ⊞	(The Start button.) To display the Start menu.
Click **All Programs**	To display the All Programs submenu.
Choose **Microsoft Office**, **Microsoft Publisher 2010**	To start Microsoft Publisher.
2 Observe the title bar	Microsoft Publisher
	You haven't created or opened a publication yet, so no publication title appears.
3 Click **Open**	(On the File tab.) The Open Publication dialog box appears.
Navigate to the current topic folder	Student Data folder Unit 1\Topic A.
4 Select **Outlander Review**	
Click **Open**	To open the selected publication.
5 Observe the title bar	Outlander Review - Microsoft Publisher
	The title bar displays the publication's name.

The Publisher window

Explanation

Publisher has several components you use to interact with the program. Exhibit 1-1 shows some of these components.

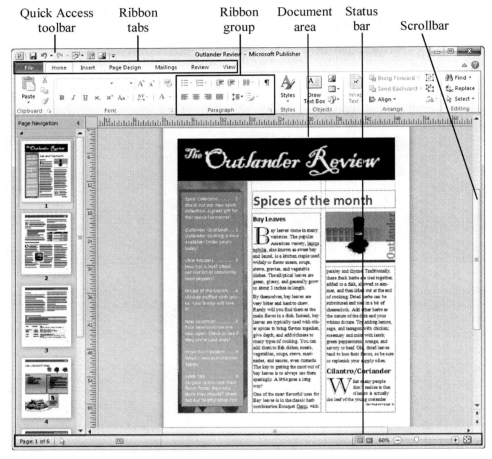

Exhibit 1-1: Components of the Publisher 2010 window

The following table describes the components of the Publisher window.

Item	Description
File tab	Opens Backstage view, which displays a menu of commonly used file-management commands, such as Open, Save As, and Print.
Quick Access toolbar	Contains buttons for frequently used commands. By default, Save, Undo, and Repeat/Redo are available. You can customize the toolbar to include additional commands.
Ribbon tabs	Contain Publisher's primary tools and commands, which are organized in logical groups and divided among the tabs. The main tabs are File, Home, Insert, Page Design, Mailings, Review, and View.
Ribbon groups	Further organize related tools and commands. For example, tools and menus for changing text formats are arranged together in the Font group.
Title bar	Displays the name of the current publication.
Scratch area	The extra space around the page that you can use for storing text and graphics. Items in the scratch area don't appear in the printed publication.
Document area	Displays the text and graphics that you type, edit, or insert. The flashing vertical line in the document area is called the insertion point, and it indicates where text will appear as you type.
Page Navigation pane	Displays thumbnails of the pages in a publication. Click to navigate to a particular page or spread. The thumbnail for the currently displayed page is highlighted.
Layout guides	Blue and red dotted lines that help you align page elements. These lines don't appear in the printed publication.
Horizontal ruler	Helps you align objects horizontally on the page. You can also use it to adjust or remove tab stops and indents.
Vertical ruler	Helps you align objects vertically on the page.
Status bar	Contains the page count, current location of the pointer or the size and position of any selected object, and the Zoom slider.
Scrollbars	Used to view parts of the publication that don't currently fit in the window. You can scroll vertically and horizontally.

The Ribbon

Publisher 2010 uses the Ribbon interface first implemented in other Office programs beginning with Office 2007. The Ribbon takes the place of menus and toolbars used in previous versions of Publisher. The Ribbon is divided into *tabs*, such as Home, Insert, and Page Design, as shown in Exhibit 1-2. Each tab displays related commands and menus, arranged in *groups*, such as Clipboard, Font, Paragraph, and so on. Within each group are commands, buttons, and menus. The size of the buttons adjusts to accommodate the size of the window.

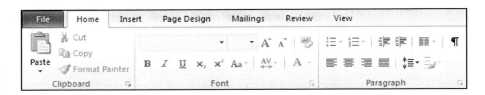

Exhibit 1-2: The Home tab (shown in two parts)

Contextual Ribbon tabs

Some Ribbon tabs remain hidden until they are needed. *Contextual tabs* appear only if the object they control is inserted or selected. For example, the Picture Tools | Format tab appears whenever you insert or select a picture.

Galleries

Many Ribbon elements include galleries. Instead of displaying a menu of things to do, a *gallery* typically displays a graphical representation of the results of a command.

Some galleries and menus in Publisher use the *Live Preview* feature. When you point to a selection in a list or gallery that provides a Live Preview, the selected text or object in the document displays the result of that selection, as shown in Exhibit 1-3.

Picture Styles gallery   Live Preview of the selected style

Pointer

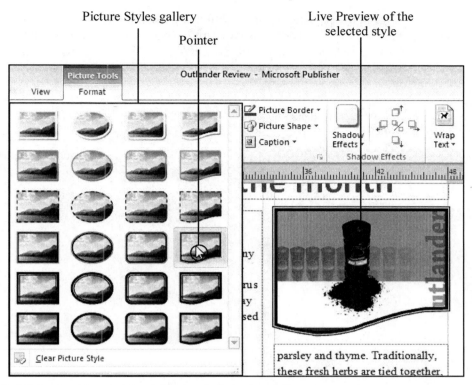

Exhibit 1-3: Live Preview for the Cell Styles gallery in Excel

Minimizing the Ribbon

The Ribbon puts commonly used commands within easy reach, but it takes up a lot of space on the screen. Some users prefer to minimize the Ribbon, as shown in Exhibit 1-4, in order to have more screen space while they're working. You can minimize the Ribbon either by clicking the Minimize the Ribbon button or by double-clicking the active tab. The Minimize the Ribbon button is the caret-shaped button to the left of the Help button, at the right end of the Ribbon.

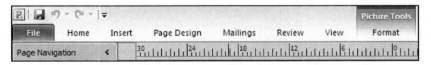

Exhibit 1-4: The Ribbon can be minimized to save screen space

Once you have minimized the Ribbon, you can click a tab to temporarily show it so you can access a command. The Ribbon will be displayed until you click a command or click elsewhere in the window. Then it will be hidden again.

To expand the Ribbon and keep it expanded, click the Expand the Ribbon button (the down-pointing caret) or double-click a tab.

The Dialog Box Launcher

In Publisher, there are more commands and settings than can be displayed on the Ribbon. Dialog boxes are available, where necessary, to display more detailed settings. To open a dialog box, click the *Dialog Box Launcher* that appears in the lower-right corner of many groups on the Ribbon, as shown in Exhibit 1-5.

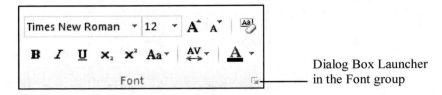

Dialog Box Launcher
in the Font group

Exhibit 1-5: The Dialog Box Launcher in the Font group

Do it!

A-2: Exploring the Publisher window

Here's how	Here's why
1 Observe the Ribbon	The Ribbon is divided into tabs, which are further organized into groups.
2 Place the insertion point in the publication	(Click on any text.) To activate all of the groups on the Home tab.
3 In the Font group, click the arrow on the right side of the Font list	 To display a list of fonts.
Press ESC	To close the Font list.
4 Click the **Drawing Tools | Format** tab	This contextual tab was displayed when you placed the mouse pointer.
In the Shape Styles group, click as shown	 (The More button.) To expand the Shape Styles gallery.
Click anywhere in the publication	To close the gallery.
5 Identify the scratch area	(The bluish-gray area surrounding the page boundaries.) You can use this area to store text and graphics. Items in the scratch area don't appear in the printed publication.
6 Identify the rulers	The horizontal and vertical rulers help you keep track of the dimensions of your publication and the position of text and graphics on the page.
Move the pointer around the page and observe the rulers	Lines on the rulers indicate the current position of the pointer.

The Quick Access toolbar

The *Quick Access toolbar* is a convenient location for frequently used commands, including Save and Undo. By default, the Quick Access toolbar is located above the Ribbon, but you can display it below the Ribbon. To do this, click the arrow on the right side of the toolbar and choose Show Below the Ribbon.

Adding a command to the Quick Access toolbar

You can customize the Quick Access toolbar to include commands or other frequently used Ribbon elements so that you can use them without having to keep switching Ribbon tabs. For example, if you work with a file that must be e-mailed to co-workers at the end of every session, you might want to place an icon for the E-mail command on the Quick Access toolbar.

You can add any elements from the Ribbon to the Quick Access toolbar so that they're always visible. You can add groups, galleries, menus, lists, and commands. To add an item to the Quick Access toolbar, right-click the item on the Ribbon and choose Add to Quick Access Toolbar. To add a dialog box, right-click the appropriate Dialog Box Launcher.

Microsoft has anticipated some commands that you might want to add. You can add them by clicking the arrow on the right side of the Quick Access toolbar and choosing the desired command from the Quick Access Toolbar menu.

Adding hidden commands to the Quick Access toolbar

You might want to use commands that don't appear anywhere in the default interface. To add a hidden command to the Quick Access toolbar:

1 Open the Customize the Quick Access Toolbar page in the Options dialog box for the application by doing either of the following:

  - From the Quick Access Toolbar menu, choose More Commands.
  - Right-click anywhere on the Ribbon or the Quick Access toolbar and choose Customize Quick Access Toolbar.

2 From the "Choose commands from" list, select the type of commands you want to see.

3 Select the desired command and click Add. The command appears in the Customize Quick Access Toolbar list.

4 Click OK.

Do it!

A-3:   Adding a command to the Quick Access toolbar

Here's how	**Here's why**
1 Click the **View** tab	You'll add a command to the Quick Access toolbar.
2 In the Window group, right-click **Switch Windows**	To display a shortcut menu for this button.
Choose **Add to Quick Access Toolbar**	
Observe the Quick Access toolbar	
	The Switch Windows button appears on the right side of the toolbar, just before the drop-down arrow.
3 In the Layout group, right-click **Two-Page Spread**	
Choose **Add to Quick Access Toolbar**	
4 Click the **Insert** tab	
5 Add the Picture button to the Quick Access toolbar	In the Illustrations group, right-click the Picture button and choose Add to Quick Access Toolbar.

Microsoft Office Backstage view

Explanation

Backstage view is where you manage your publications and related data. To display Backstage view, click the File tab. In Backstage view, you can open, save, close, print, and share files. You can also create a publication or see a list of recently opened files. In addition, you can manage information about a file. You can also change application settings or get help with using Publisher.

Publication properties

Each Publisher file stores information about the publication itself. A publication's properties are also referred to as *metadata*. To view and edit a document's properties, click Info on the File tab. Then, under the preview of the publication, click Publication Properties and select Advanced Properties.

Compatibility with older versions of Publisher

To ensure that someone with an older version of Publisher can open your files, you can change the file type. To do so, click Save & Send on the File tab; then, under File Types, click Change File Type to display the other options, as shown in Exhibit 1-6. Choose either the Publisher 2000 Publication or the Publisher 98 Publication formats. Then click Save As.

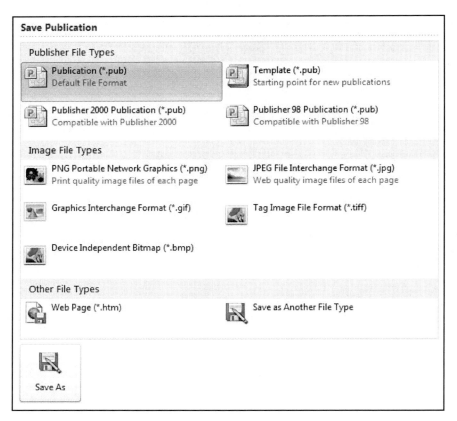

Exhibit 1-6: File type options on the File tab

Do it!

A-4: Viewing and editing publication properties

Here's how	Here's why
1 On the File tab, click **Info**	(If necessary.) To display information about the publication and its properties.
2 Under the publication preview, click **Publication Properties** and select **Advanced Properties**	To open the Outlander Review Properties dialog box.
3 In the Title box, type **Outlander Review**	
4 In the Keywords box, type **spices, recipes, newsletter**	
Click **OK**	To close the dialog box.
5 Press (ESC)	To return to the document window.
6 On the File tab, click **Close**	An alert box appears, asking if you want to save the changes you've made.
Click **Don't Save**	To close the publication.

Topic B: Navigation and selection techniques

Explanation

Knowing how to navigate a document and how to select text can save time as you work on a publication. Publisher sometimes provides several ways to accomplish a task such as zooming on a page, for example, and knowing these techniques will help you navigate the pages of a layout quickly and efficiently.

Basic navigation

By default, pages are displayed one at a time. If your publication has multiple pages and you want to view two pages at a time, click the View tab and, in the Layout group, click Two-Page Spread to display facing pages in pairs. To return to viewing pages one at a time, in the Layout group, click Single Page.

The Page Navigation pane

In Publisher, the Page Navigation pane, shown in Exhibit 1-7, displays thumbnails of publication pages. To navigate to a particular page, click its thumbnail in the Page Navigation pane. The page numbers also appear below the thumbnails. You can right-click the thumbnails to access a shortcut menu specific to the Page Navigation pane. From the shortcut menu, you can change the view, insert pages, delete pages, and more.

Exhibit 1-7: The Page Navigation pane

Do it!

B-1: Navigating pages

The files for this activity are in Student Data folder **Unit 1\Topic B**.

Here's how	Here's why
1 Open Outlander Review2	On the File tab, click Open. Navigate to the current topic folder and select the file; then click Open.
2 How many pages are there in this publication?	
3 Click the page 2 thumbnail	To view page 2.
4 Go to page 5	Click the page 5 thumbnail.
5 In the Page Navigation pane, right-click and choose **View Two-Page Spread**	To view facing pages together.

The status bar

Explanation

The status bar, at the bottom of the application window, displays information about the active file. The status bar also contains buttons you can use to switch the view, and controls you can use to zoom in and out.

Zooming with the status bar

You can view a page at different magnification levels. To do so, use any of the following techniques:

- Right-click and choose Zoom, and select a magnification from the submenu.
- On the View tab, in the Zoom group, select a magnification.
- On the status bar, click the Zoom Out and Zoom In buttons, or use the slider.

When an item on the page is selected, Publisher zooms centered on that item; otherwise, it zooms centered on the page. To fill the window with the selected object, you can select Selected Objects. By default, Publisher shows the whole page in the window.

The status bar provides three ways to zoom in and out on a document, as shown in Exhibit 1-8. You can drag the slider bar to change the magnification. You can click the Zoom Out (+) and Zoom In (–) buttons. You can also click the Show Whole Page button to fit the page in the document window.

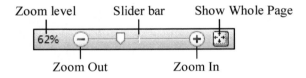

Exhibit 1-8: The Zoom buttons and slider bar

Do it!   ### B-2:   Zooming by using the status bar

Here's how	Here's why
1 Observe the right side of the status bar	At the bottom of the application window.
Point to each of the view buttons	A tooltip displays each button's name.
2 Click ▤	(The Single Page button.) To view one page at a time.
3 Drag the Zoom slider bar slightly to the left	`49%  ⊖ ──▫────── ⊕ ⊡`
	The zoom percentage changes, and the view of the page zooms out.
Click ⊞	(The Zoom In button on the slider.) To zoom in to the nearest 10%.
Zoom to 100%	Keep clicking Zoom In until the Zoom level is 100%.
4 Click ⊡	(The Show Whole Page button.) To fit the page in the document window.

Selecting text

Explanation

In Publisher, you enter text in text boxes. Aside from this difference, you can select text as you would in a word-processing program like Microsoft Word (which doesn't primarily use text boxes).

After you've selected the text, you can move it or copy it to another location within the publication or to another publication. You can delete the selected text by pressing Delete or Backspace or by typing new text to replace the selected text. By default, selected text is replaced by anything you type. So, while working with selected text, you need to be careful to avoid accidentally typing over it.

If you've selected some text, you can deselect it by doing any of the following:

- Click outside the selected text.
- Select other text.
- Press an arrow key.

Select text by using the mouse

There are several ways you can use the mouse to select text. You can drag across the text you want to select, double-click a word to select it, or use a combination of the mouse and the Shift or Ctrl keys. By default, when you're dragging to select more than one word, Publisher automatically selects entire words. This means that if you begin dragging in the middle of a word and continue dragging to select additional text, the entire first word will be selected.

The following table describes basic techniques for using the mouse to select text.

To select...	Do this
A word	Point to the word and double-click.
A paragraph	Point anywhere in the paragraph and triple-click.
A group of words	Point to the beginning of the text you want to select, press and hold the mouse button, and drag the pointer across the text. Release the mouse button to finish selecting the text.
	Alternatively, place the insertion point at the beginning or end of the text, press and hold Shift, and click at the other end of the text.

Select text by using the keyboard

You can use the arrow keys, the Home and End keys, and the Shift key to select text in your publication. The following table explains how to use the keyboard to select text.

Keys	Action
Shift+Left Arrow	Selects the text to the left of the insertion point one character at a time.
Shift+Right Arrow	Selects the text to the right of the insertion point one character at a time.
Ctrl+Shift+Left Arrow	Selects the text to the left of the insertion point one word at a time.
Ctrl+Shift+Right Arrow	Selects the text to the right of the insertion point one word at a time.
Shift+Up Arrow	Selects text from the left of the insertion point to the same position in the previous line.
Shift+Down Arrow	Selects text from the right of the insertion point to the same position in the next line.
Shift+Home	Selects text from the left of the insertion point to the beginning of the current line.
Shift+End	Selects text from the right of the insertion point to the end of the current line.
Ctrl+A	Selects the contents of the entire text box.

Do it!

B-3: Using the mouse to select text

Here's how	Here's why
1 On page 1, place the insertion point before "Bay," as shown	**Bay Leaves** Bay leaves come in many varieties. The popular American variety, laurus nobilis, also known as sweet bay Before the first word of the article, under the heading "Bay Leaves."
Drag to the end of the line, as shown	**Bay Leaves** Bay leaves come in many varieties. The popular American variety, laurus nobilis, also known as sweet bay To select a range of text.
2 Click away from the selection	To deselect the text.
3 Place the insertion point at the beginning of the paragraph	Before the word "Bay" in the first sentence.
4 Press (SHIFT) + (→)	(Hold Shift and press the Right Arrow key.) To select the first letter.
5 Press (CTRL) + (SHIFT) + (→)	To select the word "Bay."
6 Press and hold (SHIFT)	
Click anywhere below the insertion point	To select a range of text.
Click at another point below the text you've selected	(Be sure that you're pressing Shift.) To add to the selection.
Release (SHIFT)	
7 Deselect the text	Click outside of the selected text.
8 Close the publication without saving	On the File tab, click Close. In the alert box, click Don't Save.

Topic C: Publisher Help

Explanation

You can use the Help system to get program information and instructions as you work. If your system is connected to the Internet, you can find online help information as well. To do so, ensure that "Connected to Office.com" appears in the bottom-right corner of the Publisher Help window.

Getting help with Publisher 2010

To open Help, click the Microsoft Publisher Help button in the upper-right corner of the document window, or press F1. On the File tab, you can click Help for even more options, such as contacting Microsoft or checking for updates; on the File tab, click Microsoft Office Help to open the Publisher Help window.

In the Publisher Help window, shown in Exhibit 1-9, type the word or term you want to search for and press Enter. The Help system works like a web browser—each topic name is a hyperlink that, when clicked, displays information about that topic.

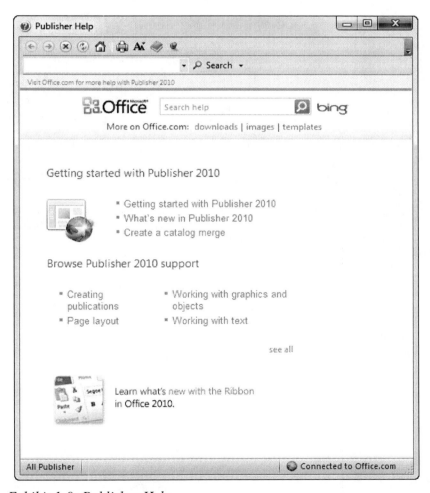

Exhibit 1-9: Publisher Help

Do it!

C-1: Using Publisher Help

Here's how	Here's why
1 In the upper-right corner of the document window, click [?]	(The Microsoft Publisher Help button.) To open Publisher Help.
2 In the Search box, type **backstage view**	
Click as shown	

> Search
> 🌐 Content from Office.com
> All Publisher
> Publisher Help
> Publisher Templates
> Publisher Training
> Developer Reference
> 💻 Content from this computer
> ✓ Publisher Help
> Developer Reference

	To display the Search options. By default, "Publisher Help" is displayed.
Click **Search**	To close the menu and search for Help topics containing the phrase "backstage view."
3 In the search results list, click **What and where is Backstage view**	To display information about that topic.
4 Close Publisher Help	(Click the Close button in the upper-right corner of the Publisher Help window.) To return to Publisher.

Unit summary: Getting started

Topic A In this topic, you learned how to **start Publisher** and **open a publication**. You also learned about the **Ribbon** and the **Quick Access toolbar**. You also learned how to use **Backstage view**.

Topic B In this topic, you learned how to **navigate** a publication and how to **zoom** in and out. You also learned how to **select text**.

Topic C In this topic, you used **Publisher Help** to search for information on a specific topic.

Independent practice activity

In this activity, you'll view different task panes and toolbars. Then you'll open a publication and navigate its pages. Finally, you'll use help.

The files for this activity are in Student Data folder **Unit 1\Unit summary**.

1 Open **Outlander Review**.

2 Go to page 3.

3 Change the view so that Publisher displays two pages at a time.

4 Change the zoom level to **75%**.

5 Change the zoom level to display the entire page in the document window.

6 Change the view so that Publisher displays one page at a time.

7 Get help on **customizing toolbars**. When you're done, close the Publisher Help window.

8 View the publication properties.

9 In the Author field, enter your name.

10 Close the publication without saving. (When you're prompted to save changes, click Don't Save.)

Review questions

1 Which feature of the Publisher interface is divided into tabs and groups, and contains menus, commands, and lists?

A File tab

B Ribbon

C Quick Access toolbar

D Status bar

2 Which Publisher feature resembles a list but displays a graphical representation of the result of an action?

A Contextual tabs

B Ribbon lists

C Galleries

D Dialog Box Launchers

3 How can you modify publication properties?

4 How can you zoom in on a page?

A Right-click and choose Zoom, and select a magnification from the submenu

B On the View tab, in the Zoom group, select a magnification

C On the status bar, click the Zoom Out and Zoom In buttons, or use the slider

D All of the above

5 What is the keyboard shortcut for selecting a word to the right of the insertion point?

A Shift+Right Arrow

B Ctrl+Shift+Right Arrow

C Shift+Home

D Shift+End

6 How can you access online help for questions with Publisher?

Unit 2

Basic publications

Unit time: 60 minutes

Complete this unit, and you'll know how to:

A Create a new publication and add basic elements to a layout.

B Position elements precisely by using guides and the Measurement task pane.

Topic A: Publication basics

Explanation

In Publisher, you can create single-page publications, such as flyers that promote a sale, or multi-page publications, such as a company's employee newsletter or a product information document.

Publication templates

When you start Publisher, the New section of the File tab displays the available templates you can use to start creating a publication. You can start with a template that includes elements such as text boxes and graphics placeholders, and then modify these by replacing them with your own content. You also can start with a blank publication template and add these elements yourself.

To create a new blank, single-page, letter-sized (8.5" × 11") publication, click the File tab, and then click New to view the available templates; click the Blank 8.5 × 11" template. Otherwise, click a template category to view the templates available. To view all available templates, make sure to select "Installed and Online Templates" from the drop-down list at the top of the window.

If you work mostly by creating publications from scratch, you can specify that Publisher creates a new blank document when you start it, rather than with the template gallery. To do so, click the File tab and click Options to open the Publisher Options dialog box. In the General section, under Start up options, clear "Show the New template gallery when starting Publisher."

Margin guides

Blue lines called *margin guides* delineate a publication's margins. Margin guides appear on the top, bottom, and sides of each page in a publication. Margin guides can help you to visualize the boundary for page content as well as to position page elements. Margin guides do not appear in the final printed publication.

You can select a predefined setting for margin guides by clicking the Page Design tab and, in the Page Setup group, clicking Margins.

You can also specify custom margins. To do so:

1 Click the Page Design tab.
2 Click Margins and select Custom Margins to open the Layout Guides dialog box, shown in Exhibit 2-1.
3 Click the Margin Guides tab, if necessary.
4 Under Margin Guides, edit the Left, Right, Top, and Bottom boxes as necessary. The Preview section shows what the margins will look like in the publication.
5 Click OK.

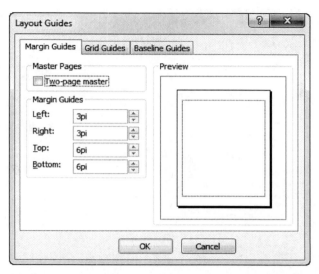

Exhibit 2-1: The Margin Guides tab in the Layout Guides dialog box

Units of measurement

In Publisher, inches are the default unit of measurement. However, the traditional measurement system used in typesetting includes *picas* and *points*. Font size, for example, is often measured in points. Print designers and typesetters today typically use the picas and points measurement system. If you're new to the picas and points measurement system, the following conversions might be helpful:

- 72 points = 1 inch
- 12 points = 1 pica
- 6 picas = 1 inch

To set a publication to use picas as the unit of measure:

1 Click the File tab.
2 Click Options to open the Publisher Options dialog box, shown in Exhibit 2-2.
3 Click Advanced.
4 Under Display, from the "Show measurements in units of" list, select Picas.
5 Click OK.

Publisher uses a shorthand notation to denote values using the picas and points measurement system. Picas are represented by "pi," and points are represented as "pt." For example, if you specify a margin of 3 picas, the value will appear as 3 pi; if you specify a value 12 points, it will appear as 12 pt.

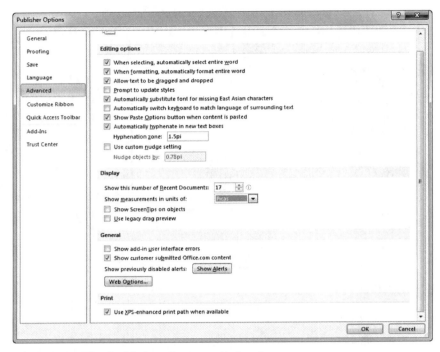

Exhibit 2-2: The Publisher Options dialog box

Saving a publication

To save a publication, click the File tab and click Save. If the publication has not yet been saved, the Save As dialog box opens. Navigate to the location where you want to save the file, and then enter a file name in the File name box and click Save. If the publication was saved previously, then clicking Save on the File tab will update the publication with any changes you've made. You also can press Ctrl+S to update a publication, or you can click the Save icon on the Quick Access toolbar.

Do it!

A-1: Creating a new publication

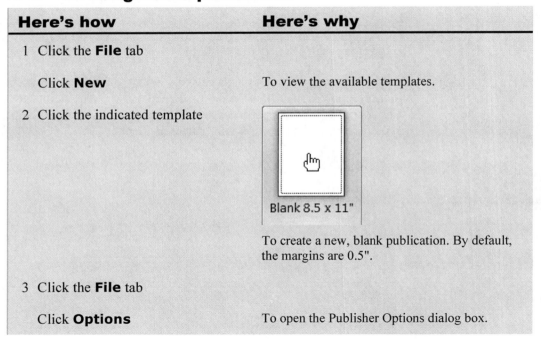

Here's how	Here's why
1 Click the **File** tab	
Click **New**	To view the available templates.
2 Click the indicated template	
	Blank 8.5 x 11"
	To create a new, blank publication. By default, the margins are 0.5".
3 Click the **File** tab	
Click **Options**	To open the Publisher Options dialog box.

4   Click **Advanced**

Under Display, from the "Show
measurements in units of" list,
select **Picas**

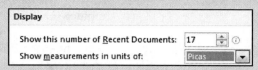

A pica is a unit of measurement used in print
publishing.

Click **OK**

To close the dialog box.

5   Locate the margin guides on the
page

The blue lines in the document indicate the top,
left, right, and bottom margins.

6   Click the **Page Design** tab

To open the Layout Guides dialog box.

In the Page Setup group, click
Margins

Select **Custom Margins...**

To open the Layout Guides dialog box.

7   On the Top box, click the up
arrow until the value reads **6pi**

Set the Bottom margin to **6pi**

Click the **Grid Guides** tab

Edit the Columns box to read **2**

To create column guides in the layout.

Click **OK**

The margin guides adjust accordingly.

8   Click the **File** tab

Click **Save**

The Save As dialog box appears. This
publication has not yet been saved, so you're
prompted by the Save As dialog box to give it a
name.

Navigate to the current topic
folder

Edit the File name box to read
My recipe layout 1

Click **Save**

To save the publication.

Text boxes

Explanation

Publisher uses *text boxes* to place and arrange all the text in a layout. You can use text boxes to place text exactly where you want on a page, and you can use separate text boxes for different text elements. For example, if you have more than one article on a page (as in a magazine or newspaper), you can place each article in its own text box. This allows you to position and size each article independently.

To create a text box, on the Home tab, in the Objects group, click Draw Text Box, and then drag the pointer anywhere on the page. (You can also click Draw Text Box in the Text group on the Insert tab.) After you create a text box, you can adjust its size and position as needed:

- Point to the text box border until the pointer displays a four-sided arrow, then drag to move the text box as needed.
- Drag the handles on the text box to resize it.

To insert text in a text box, place the insertion point in the text box and type. You can also insert text from an external file. When working with a text box, the Drawing Tools | Format and the Text Box Tools | Format tabs appear. You can use these to specify formatting settings for the text box as well as for the text within it.

Displaying boundaries

When you add an element such as a text box, shape, or picture to a page, its boundaries indicate where the edges of the object are. By default, Publisher doesn't show these boundaries unless the object is selected. To show boundaries for all objects on a page, on the View tab, in the Show group, check Boundaries.

Selecting text

Any character formatting you specify will be applied only to the selected text. There are several ways you can select text for editing or formatting.

- Click twice on a word to select the whole word.
- Click three times anywhere in a paragraph to select that paragraph.
- Press Ctrl+A to select all of the text in a text box.

Character formatting

You can draw a reader's attention to specific parts of a publication and improve its overall readability by applying character formatting. Character formats include fonts, font sizes, and font styles. Although it's not a good idea to use many different formats in a single document, it is generally good practice to use different fonts and text sizes for headlines and body text, for example. Likewise, you might apply italics to indicate emphasis or apply boldface to set off a subheading.

You can apply character formatting by using the options in the Font dialog box. Many of those options are also available in the Font group, which is on both the Home tab and the Text Box Tools | Format tab, shown in Exhibit 2-3. In addition, when you select text, the Mini toolbar appears above it. The Mini toolbar includes some of the formatting options in the Font and Paragraph groups.

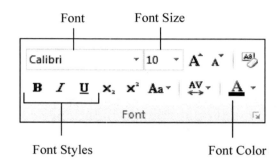

Exhibit 2-3: Text formatting options in the Font group

Fonts and font sizes

The font and size of text can greatly affect its readability, and different kinds of fonts are typically used for different purposes. For example, an elegant script font would be appropriate for a wedding invitation but not for a business letter. Two commonly used fonts are Times New Roman and Arial. Publisher 2010 uses Calibri as the default font for new text boxes.

Fonts can be categorized in various ways, such as by their typical use or by certain design characteristics. Two categories based on the latter are serif and sans serif.

A *serif* font, such as Times New Roman, has small lines at the top and bottom of its letters. (Think of the bottom ones as small feet.) A serif font often works well on a printed page with large blocks of text because the lines help lead the reader's eyes across the page. A *sans serif* font, such as Arial, lacks the small lines of a serif font. A sans serif font works well for headings because the streamlined letter shapes make the text easy to read at a glance.

Font styles

Font styles (also called typestyles) include italic, bold, and underlined. You can emphasize a specific word or phrase by using these styles. For example, using boldface text in headings helps draw a reader's attention to important information. In addition, the bold heading format helps the reader see the document's sections and structure, making the information easier to read and absorb.

One way to apply font styles is to select the desired text and use the Bold, Italic, or Underline buttons in the Font group. You can also use the keyboard.

The following table shows the font styles and the buttons and keyboard shortcuts used to apply them.

Style	Button	Keyboard shortcut
Bold	**B**	Ctrl+B
Italic	*I*	Ctrl+I
Underline	U	Ctrl+U

Removing font styles

To remove all font styles applied to text, select the text and press Ctrl+Spacebar.

Do it!

A-2: Creating text in a publication

Here's how	Here's why
1 On the Home tab, in the Objects group, click **Draw Text Box**	You'll create a large heading near the top of the page.
2 Point near the top of the page and drag down and to the right, as shown	To create a new text box.
Observe the new text box	The insertion point appears inside the text box, indicating that you can add text to it.
3 Type **Spicy Buzzard Wings**	You'll make the text bigger and apply a different font.
4 Press CTRL + A	To select all the text in the text box.
On the Text Box Tools | Format tab, in the Font group, observe the Font and Font Size settings	Calibri 10 You'll increase the size of the text.
5 From the Size list, select **36**	

6 In the Font group, click [**B**]   (The Bold button.) To make the text bold.

7 Observe the text box

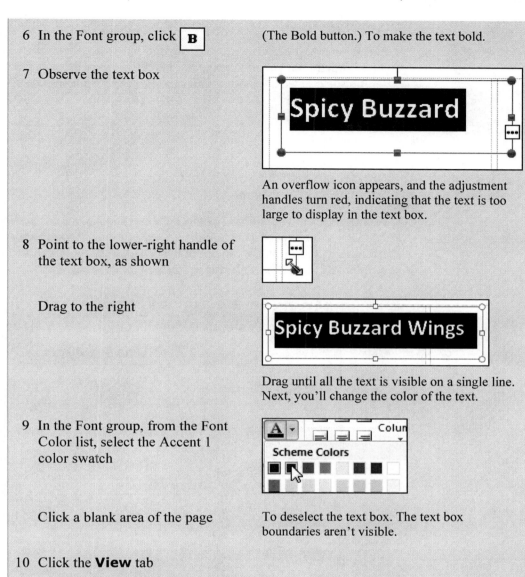

An overflow icon appears, and the adjustment handles turn red, indicating that the text is too large to display in the text box.

8 Point to the lower-right handle of the text box, as shown

Drag to the right

Drag until all the text is visible on a single line. Next, you'll change the color of the text.

9 In the Font group, from the Font Color list, select the Accent 1 color swatch

Click a blank area of the page   To deselect the text box. The text box boundaries aren't visible.

10 Click the **View** tab

Check **Boundaries**   To view the boundaries for shapes, text boxes, and pictures.

11 Press (CTRL) + (S)   To update the publication.

Inserting text

Explanation

You can enter text directly into your layout, but you'll most likely need to insert text that has already been written and edited in another application, such as Microsoft Word. After you've created a text box, you can insert text from another file, such as a word processing document:

1 Place the insertion point inside the text box where you want to place the text.

2 On the Insert tab, in the Text group, click Insert File to open the Insert Text dialog box.

3 Navigate to the file you want to insert.

4 Click OK to insert the text.

If you insert a file without first placing the insertion point in an existing text box, Publisher will create a text box automatically. If the text you're placing overflows Publisher's default text box, then Publisher will create a linked text box on a separate page. You'll learn about linked text boxes in another activity.

Do it!

A-3: Inserting text in a publication

The files for this activity are in Student Data folder **Unit 2\Topic A**.

Here's how	Here's why
1 Click the **Insert** tab	You'll create a new text box and populate it with text inserted from a Microsoft Word document.
In the Text group, click **Draw Text Box**	
Create a text box in the left column below the display text, as shown	**Spicy Buzzard Wings**
	Publisher snaps the text box to the column guides when you drag close to them.
	The insertion point flashes inside the new text box, so you're ready to insert text.

2 On the Insert tab, in the Text group, click **Insert File** — To open the Insert Text dialog box.

   Select **Ingredients** — In the current topic folder.

   Click **OK** — To insert the text from the Microsoft Word document into the text box.

   Verify that the text doesn't overflow — Resize the text box, if necessary.

3 Create a similar box in the right column, as shown

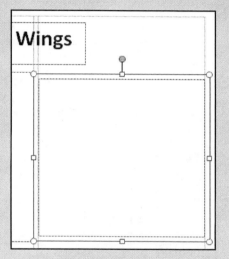

4 Insert **Directions** into the new text box — On the Insert tab, in the Text group, click Insert File, and then select Directions and click OK.

   Verify that the text doesn't overflow — Resize the text box, if necessary.

5 Update the publication — Press Ctrl+S.

Pictures

Explanation

Pictures enhance the look of a publication. Varying the sizes of your pictures can help readers discern which items in a publication are most important and can enhance the flow and readability of your publication.

Inserting pictures is similar to inserting text. You can insert a picture in a frame you have already drawn, or you can have Publisher automatically create a frame when you insert the picture. To insert a picture in an existing frame:

1   On the Insert tab, in the Illustrations group, click Picture Placeholder. Publisher creates a default picture frame in the layout and activates the Picture Tools | Format tab.

2   Adjust the size of the picture frame as desired.

3   In the Insert group, click Picture to open the Insert Picture dialog box.

4   Select the desired file and click Insert. The picture appears in the picture frame, scaled to fit the frame. In addition, the Crop handles are active.

5   If necessary, reposition or resize the picture within the frame, dragging it or its selection handles.

Resizing pictures

When you resize a graphic, you should be cautious about increasing the size. Sometimes increasing a graphic's size too much can significantly degrade its appearance. However, you can typically decrease a graphic's size without degrading its appearance. After resizing graphics significantly, you might want to print a test copy of the document to ensure that you get the results you expect.

To resize a graphic:

- Drag one of the four corner resize handles to resize the image proportionally.
- Drag the resize handles on the top, bottom, or sides of the picture to stretch the image. For example, drag the top handle to stretch the image vertically, without changing the horizontal dimension.
- Press Ctrl and drag any of the resize handles to resize the image from the center point of the picture.

You can also resize a graphic by entering a specific percentage. To do so:

1   Right-click the graphic and choose Format Picture.

2   In the Format Picture dialog box, click the Size tab.

3   Under Scale, in the Height and Width boxes, enter new percentages. Click OK.

Rotating pictures

As with resizing graphics, you can rotate a graphic by dragging it or by entering a value in a dialog box.

To rotate a graphic manually:

1   Select the graphic.

2   Point to the green rotation handle at the top of the graphic. The pointer changes to a rotating arrow.

3   Drag to rotate the graphic.

To rotate a graphic numerically:

1   Right-click the graphic and choose Format Picture.

2   In the Format Picture dialog box, click the Size tab.

3   Under Rotate, in the Rotation box, enter the rotation value you want to use. Click OK.

Cropping pictures

When you place a picture in an existing frame, Publisher activates the Crop handles, as shown in Exhibit 2-4. This allows you to modify the size of the frame, the picture's position within the frame, and the size of the picture independent of the frame it's within. To turn the Crop handles on or off, on the Picture Tools | Format tab, in the Crop group, click Crop.

You also can adjust how the picture fills its frame. In the Crop group, click Fit to have the entire picture displayed in the frame. Click Fill to have the picture fill the frame— Publisher will scale it to fill the frame boundary, probably resulting in some of the picture being cropped. Finally, click Clear Crop to have the picture frame adjust to match the edges of the picture.

When you click Crop, you can move the picture within the frame, for example, to display a specific part of a larger image. You also can modify the frame boundaries. When the Crop handles aren't active, you can use the adjustment handles to resize the picture and its frame together.

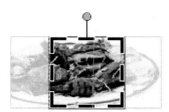

Exhibit 2-4: Crop handles activated for a picture

When you insert a picture without first specifying an existing frame, Publisher places the picture in a new frame that matches the size of the original picture.

Changing the stacking order

As you add pictures and text, the frames might overlap each other. By default, each new frame you create is positioned at the top of the stacking order. This means that new objects will overlap existing ones. However, you might want an object that is in front of another object to appear behind it.

To change the stacking order, begin by selecting an object. Then, in the Arrange group, click either Bring Forward or Send Backward and choose the command you want: Bring Forward, Bring to Front, Send Backward, or Send to Back. The Bring Forward and Send Backward commands move objects forward or backward one position in the stacking order. The Bring to Front and Send to Back commands move objects to the front of or behind all other objects.

Picture formats

You can insert many types of images. For layouts intended for print, TIFF images often give the best results and the most flexibility. Graphics formats used on the Web, such as JPEG and GIF, generally aren't suitable for commercial printing but are fine for online use. If you work with Adobe Photoshop, you won't be able to insert PSD images, so you'll have to save them in a different format.

Do it!

A-4: Inserting pictures into a publication

The files for this activity are in Student Data folder **Unit 2\Topic A**.

Here's how	Here's why
1 On Insert tab, in the Illustrations group, click **Picture Placeholder**	To create a square placeholder frame in the center of the page. Publisher activates the Picture Tools | Format tab.
2 In the Insert group, click **Picture**	To open the Insert Picture dialog box.
Select **Spicy buzzard wings**	In the current topic folder.
Click **Insert**	To insert the image into the picture frame. The picture is resized to fill the frame, and the Crop handles are active. You'll resize the picture and the frame.
3 In the Crop group, click **Clear Crop**	To resize the frame to fit the image.
In the Crop group, click **Crop**	To turn off the Crop handles.
4 Drag the bottom-right handle as shown

Place chicken wings in a large baking dish. Bake 30 minutes or until chicken wings are fork-tender.

Place chicken wings on platter. Garnish with celery. |
| | To resize the picture. |

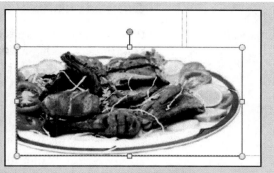

5 Drag the picture so that it lines up with the left and bottom page margins, as shown

Next, you'll insert a picture at actual size, instead of having it scale to fit an existing picture frame.

6 In the Insert group, click **Picture**   To open the Insert Picture dialog box.

   Select **Coriander**

   Click **Insert**   To insert the picture into a picture frame at actual size.

7 Move the image to the pasteboard to the right of the page

8 Insert **Cinnamon** at actual size   In the Insert group, click Picture. Select the file and click Insert.

   Drag the image to the pasteboard below the coriander image

9 Insert **Nutmeg** at actual size

   Drag the image to the pasteboard below the cinnamon image

10 Update the publication

Custom colors

Explanation

If your organization has a logo or standardized colors, you can include those colors in your project. Using a custom color gives separate projects a common element and brands your publications with your organization's look and feel. To create a custom text color, you can use the Colors dialog box, shown in Exhibit 2-5.

1   On the Home tab, in the Font group, click the Font Color list and select More Colors to open the Colors dialog box.

2   Click the Custom tab.

3   Select a color model from the Color model list. For print, use CMYK. For online publishing, use RGB. Publisher also uses the HSL model, which you can use to define a color by hue, saturation, and luminosity.

4   Enter percentages for the color channels (for example, Cyan, Magenta, Yellow, and Black) or use the color picker and/or slider to choose a color.

5   Click OK to create the color and apply it to any selected text.

After you've defined a custom color, its color swatch appears in the Fill Color, Line Color, and Font Color lists.

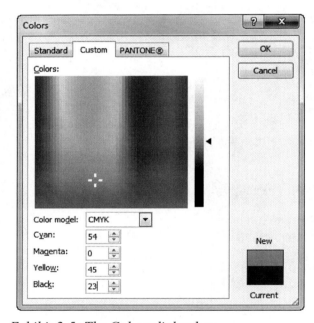

Exhibit 2-5: The Colors dialog box

Color models

Publisher uses three color models to produce colors: RGB, HSL, and CMYK. When producing publications for the Web or for print, you'll work primarily with the RGB and CMYK color models.

Computer monitors use the RGB color model to produce colors. However, when a document is printed, colors are generated differently:

- RGB color is referred to as "additive": It's much like shining colored flashlights on a black wall—the more of each component color you *add*, the greater the intensity of the color. The RGB color mode is capable of creating very bright, saturated colors, because the light colors are projected.

- CMYK color is "subtractive": Increasing a color component on a white page *subtracts* from the brightness of the color. For example, mixing cyan (a light greenish-blue) and yellow inks creates a darker color (green). Unlike with RGB color, in which the surface you view *is* the light source, when you view CMYK printed materials, you're viewing light from elsewhere reflecting off the paper.

Desktop printers are often referred to as *composite printers* because they combine CMYK inks—also referred to as *process colors*—directly onto paper to produce a range of colors. Inkjet printers, laser printers, and color copiers fall into this category. However, even though desktop printers use CMYK inks, they often use two or more additional inks to produce a wider range of colors. So you'll get best results when printing to a desktop printer by defining colors and images in RGB format.

A commercial printing press differs from a desktop printer by producing color documents using *color separations*, which are grayscale representations of each process color. For this reason, any publication that you send to be printed on a commercial press should use the CMYK color model; otherwise, you might end up with unexpected results, because the RGB colors have to be "translated" in order to print in CMYK. Some print vendors might even reject a publication submitted with RGB colors.

The process of preparing a document by separating it into color plates is called *prepress*. Traditionally, each ink color is printed on a separate piece of film, with levels of gray representing the shades of that color; then light is shone through the film to produce a color plate. A printing press then transfers the image from the plate to paper.

Do it!

A-5:   Defining a custom color

Here's how	Here's why
1 Select the text **Spicy Buzzard Wings**	You'll apply a custom color to this text.
2 From the Font Color list, select **More Colors...**	(On the Home tab, in the Font group.) To open the Colors dialog box.
3 Click the Custom tab	If necessary.
From the Color model list, select **CMYK**	CMYK is the color model used for print publications.
4 Edit the Cyan box to read **55**	
Edit the Magenta box to read **0**	
Edit the Yellow box to read **45**	
Edit the Black box to read **50**	
Click **OK**	To apply the color to the text.
5 View the Font Color list	
	The color you defined appears as a swatch in the list, under Recent Colors.
6 Deselect the text	To view the new heading color.
7 Update and close the publication	

Topic B: Object positioning

Explanation
Some designers use the "eyeball" method to place objects in a layout, arranging them until they look good to the eye. But you'll probably find that you can achieve greater consistency—and ultimately save time—by using guides, the Measurement task pane, and the align and distribute commands to align or position objects precisely.

Arranging objects by using guides

To create guides, drag them from the horizontal and vertical rulers onto the page. In addition, you can create guides by selecting an option from the Guides gallery, found in the Layout group on the Page Design tab. To align an object to a guide, drag the object so that it snaps to the guide.

In Publisher 2010, when you move an object, the new object alignment technology visually indicates how the object aligns with the margins, guides, or other objects in the layout. Guides appear as you drag an object to indicate whether it aligns with the top, bottom, sides, or center of other objects or with other guides on the page, as shown in Exhibit 2-6.

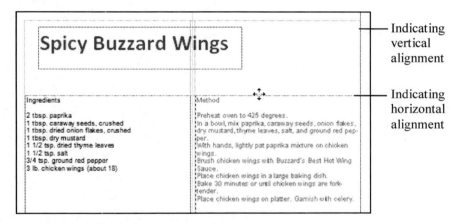

Exhibit 2-6: Object alignment guides

Moving objects

To move an object such as a picture, text box, or shape, point to it until you see the Move pointer, shown in Exhibit 2-7. Then drag the object where you want it in the layout. For text boxes, point to any boundary of the text box until you see the Move pointer.

Exhibit 2-7: The Move pointer

Show and hide guides

Sometimes you might want to preview a page without the guides showing, to see it as it will appear in print. To temporarily show or hide guides, on the View tab, in the Show group, check or clear Guides.

Do it!

B-1: Aligning objects to guides

The files for this activity are in Student Data folder **Unit 2\Topic B**.

Here's how	Here's why
1 Open Recipe layout 2	
Save the publication as **My recipe layout 2**	On the File tab, click Save As. Edit the File name box to read My newsletter 2, and navigate to the current topic folder. Click Save.
2 Right-click anywhere on the page	To access the context menu.
Choose **Zoom, 150%**	To zoom in on the document.
3 Point to any position on the vertical ruler	Create Vertical Guide. Shift+Drag to move vertical ruler You'll create a vertical guide.
Drag to the right	
Observe the status bar	Page: 1 of 1 ☐ 1.38, 0.00 pi. At the bottom-left of the Publisher window. The guide's precise position appears.
4 Position the new guide at the **25.5-pica** mark on the horizontal ruler	(You can verify the position by observing the status bar.) To place the guide in the center of the page, which is 51 picas wide. The new vertical guide appears in the center of the existing column guide.
5 Scroll up	To view the top of the page.
6 Point to the horizontal ruler and drag down	To create a horizontal guide.
Position the new guide at the **16.5-pica** mark on the vertical ruler	You'll use this guide to position the ingredients and cooking directions text.
7 Right-click anywhere on the page	
Choose **Zoom, Whole Page**	To view the entire page.

8 Drag the large picture frame at the bottom of the page to the right	As you drag, object alignment guides indicate alignment with objects in the layout. The first guide to appear indicates alignment with the center of the text box at the top of the page.

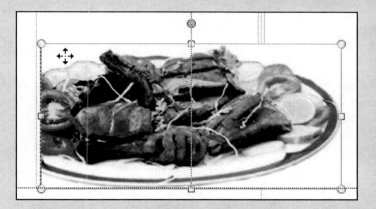

Drag the picture right to align it in the center of the page	Center the picture with the guide you created, between the column guides.

9 Point to the top boundary of the Ingredients text box	The pointer changes to the Move pointer.
Align the Ingredients text box with the horizontal guide, as shown	

Drag to align the top edge of the text box with the horizontal guide you created.

10 Align the Method text box with the horizontal guide	
11 Resize the heading text box so that it extends to the left and right margin guides	Select it, and then drag the selection handles until the boundaries snap to the margin guides.
12 Update the publication	

Arranging objects by using the Measurement task pane

Explanation

You can also position elements directly by entering values. Select an object, and then enter values in the x and y boxes in the Measurement task pane, shown in Exhibit 2-8. To view the Measurement task pane, select a text box; then, on the Drawing Tools | Format tab, in the Size box, click Measurement. The Measurement task pane can be used to position any object in a layout. The x-coordinate positions the left edge of an object relative to the horizontal ruler, and the y-coordinate positions the top edge of an object relative to the vertical ruler.

For example, assume that you have guides at the 12-pica mark on both the horizontal and vertical rulers. If you want to place the top-left corner of a text box at the intersection of the guides, you would enter 12 in both the x and y boxes in the Measurement task pane, and then press Enter.

You can also use the arrow keys to nudge an element to a desired position. When you use an arrow key to nudge an object, its position moves a fraction of a pica. (The exact amount that it moves depends on the zoom level you're using.)

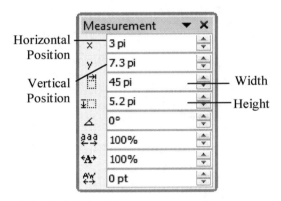

Exhibit 2-8: The Measurement task pane

Do it!

B-2:   Positioning objects precisely

Here's how	Here's why
1 Position the three small images as shown	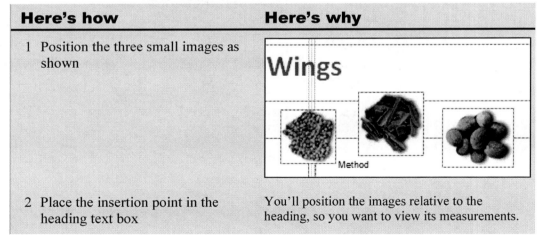
2 Place the insertion point in the heading text box	You'll position the images relative to the heading, so you want to view its measurements.

3 On the Drawing Tools | Format tab, in the Size box, click **Measurement**

Measurement	▼ ✕
x	3 pi
y	7.3 pi
⊢⊣	45 pi
⌶	5.2 pi
∠	0°
ǎaǎ⇄	100%
⁺A⁺	100%
AⱽV⇄	0 pt

To view the Measurement task pane. The left edge of the text box is aligned with the 3-pica mark on the horizontal ruler.

Drag the text box up

To align its top edge with the top page margin. The y value in the Measurement task pane changes to 6 pi.

4 Point to each value in the task pane

To identify each variable. The fourth box from the top is the Height box.

Edit the Height box to read **4** and press (↵ ENTER)

By specifying a height, you now can determine the position of the bottom edge of the text box, which could be helpful for placing other objects in the layout. The bottom edge of the text box is at 10 picas on the vertical ruler (6 pi + 4 pi).

5 Select the coriander image

You'll place the image at the 10-pica mark on the vertical ruler.

6 In the Measurement task pane, edit the x box to read **25.5**

(The x box is the horizontal position.) To set the left edge of the picture frame to 25.5 picas from the left edge of the page, aligning it with the vertical guide (the center of the page).

7 Edit the y box to read **10** and press (TAB)

To set the top edge of the picture frame to 10 picas from the top margin and aligned with the text box above it.

8 Close the Measurement palette

Click the Close button in the top-right corner of the palette.

9 Update the publication

Next, you'll align and distribute the other two spice images relative to the one you've positioned.

Alignment and distribution

Explanation

To position multiple objects relative to one another, you can use Publisher's align and distribute commands. Aligning and distributing objects can help give your layout a professional and consistent appearance. To align and distribute objects, select more than one object, and then, on the Home tab, in the Arrange group, click Align and select a command from the menu. The following table explains the available commands.

Command	Description
Align Left	Aligns the left edges of the selected objects with the left edge of the object that's farthest to the left.
Align Center	Aligns the center of the selected objects vertically.
Align Right	Aligns the right edges of the selected objects with the right edge of the object that's farthest to the right.
Align Top	Aligns the top edges of the selected objects with the top edge of the object that's farthest up on the page.
Align Middle	Aligns the centers of the selected objects horizontally.
Align Bottom	Aligns the bottom edges of the selected objects with the bottom edge of the object that's farthest down on the page.
Distribute Horizontally	Spaces the selected objects evenly horizontally.
Distribute Vertically	Spaces the selected objects evenly vertically.

To align and distribute objects relative to the page's margin guides, rather than relative to selected objects, select Relative to Margin Guides from the Align menu. Then, choose a command from the Align menu to align the objects relative to the margins. This command can be used to align a single selected object.

Do it!   **B-3:   Aligning and distributing objects**

Here's how	Here's why
1 Arrange the other two spice images as shown	
	Position the other two images lower than the coriander, and align the nutmeg image with the right margin. You want to align the tops of the images relative to the coriander image, and you want to distribute them evenly between the center of the page and the right margin.
	Notice that text automatically wraps around an object if the object overlaps it.
2 Click a blank area of the layout	To deselect all objects.
3 Press and hold `CTRL`	
Click each spice image	To select all three images.
Release `CTRL`	
4 Click the **Picture Tools | Format** tab	
In the Arrange group, click **Align** and choose **Align Top**	To align the tops of each image with the top of the highest image—in this case, the coriander image.
5 Click **Align** and choose **Distribute Horizontally**	To space the images evenly horizontally.
6 Update the publication	
On the File tab, click **Close**	To close the publication.

Unit summary: Basic publications

Topic A   In this topic, you learned how to **create a publication**. You learned how to adjust **margin guides** and set **units of measurement**. You also created text boxes, selected and formatted **text, inserted text from a file**, and moved and resized text boxes. Then you learned how to insert a picture in a frame and how to modify a **picture**. You also learned the basics of **color methods** and how to create and apply **custom colors**.

Topic B   In this topic, you learned how to **arrange objects** on a page by using **guides** and by using the **Measurement task pane**. You also learned how to **align** and **distribute** objects relative to each other and relative to guides.

Independent practice activity

In this activity, you'll create a new publication and set margins for the layout. Then you'll create and format a text box, create a custom color, and insert a photo into a picture frame.

The files for this activity are in Student Data folder **Unit 2\Unit summary**.

1 Create a new blank publication and save it as **My note 1**.

2 Set the margins for the publication as follows: Top margin: **12 picas**; Left and Right margins: **6 picas**; Bottom margin: **3 picas**. (*Hint*: First, set the measurement units to picas.)

3 Create a new text box for a headline and type **Note from the President**. Format the text as **Times New Roman, 48 point, italic**.

4 Resize the text box to align with the left and right page margin guides.

5 Create a new custom color of your choice. Apply the new color to the heading text. (*Hint*: Darker colors show up best.)

6 Insert the **President** image.

7 Create another text box and insert **President text**. Adjust the text box as necessary so that all the text is visible. (*Hint*: If you don't create a text box first, Publisher will create one on the current page and link it to another on a second page.)

8 Insert the three small spice images (Cinnamon, Coriander, and Nutmeg).

9 Arrange the elements as shown in Exhibit 2-9. Create guides to help position the elements, use the object alignment guides, and/or use the align and distribute commands.

10 Update and close the publication.

Exhibit 2-9: The publication after completing step 9

Review questions

1 When you create a new publication, there are visible guidelines on all four sides of each page that you can use to help position elements on a page. What are these called?

2 A colleague has given you measurements for a layout in inches, but you've been working with picas. How many picas are in an inch?

3 To enter text on a page, you simply click the page to place the insertion point and then begin typing, as you would in a word processor program. True or false?

4 Which image format is typically best for print publications?

   A TIFF   C PCD

   B GIF   D JPEG

5 When creating a custom color, you can choose the color model to use. Which color model is most appropriate for print publications?

6 How can you position objects precisely on a layout, by specifying x and y values as well as height and width?

Unit 3

Multi-page publications

Unit time: 45 minutes

Complete this unit, and you'll know how to:

A Create a facing-pages layout, insert pages, and move items between publications.

B Create master pages and apply them to a layout.

Topic A: Multi-page layouts

Explanation

You can create publications with either individual or facing pages. By default, Publishers Blank 8.5 × 11" template creates publications with individual pages. However, many publications that will be printed and bound, such as magazines, books, and newsletters, are designed with a facing-pages layout.

Facing pages

A facing-pages layout is designed for the pages to be bound at the center. Any bound publication that requires the reader to flip through the pages requires this kind of layout. One page is to the left of the binding, and the other is to the right, forming what's called a *spread*. The place where the bound pages meet—the inside of the spread—is called the *gutter*. A spread is always visible as a unit, so a publication that has facing pages should be designed so that each pair of pages functions as a spread, as illustrated in Exhibit 3-1. By viewing spreads, you can better coordinate elements on both pages.

To set a publication to display spreads:

1   On the Page Design tab, in the Page Setup group, click Margins and choose Custom Margins to open the Layout Guides dialog box.

2   On the Margin Guides tab, check Two-page master. The Left and Right boxes change to Inside and Outside to reflect a facing-pages layout, and the Preview box shows what a spread in the publication will look like.

3   Click OK.

4   On the View tab, in the Layout group, click Two-Page Spread.

If the publication has only one page, you won't see any difference in the layout. You can verify that it will use facing pages by pressing Ctrl+M to view the master pages.

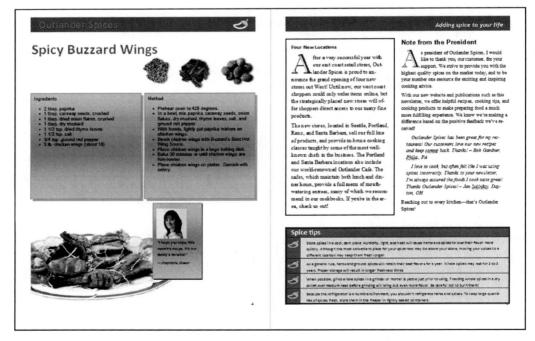

Exhibit 3-1: An example of a spread

Do it!   **A-1:   Creating a facing-pages publication**

Here's how	Here's why
1 On the File tab, click **New**	To view the available templates.
Click **Blank 8.5 × 11"**	
2 On the File tab, click **Options**	To open the Options dialog box.
Click **Advanced**	
From the "Show measurements in units of" list, select **Picas**	
Click **OK**	
3 On the Page Design tab, in the Page Setup group, click **Margins** and select **Custom Margins...**	To open the Layout Guides dialog box.
On the Margin Guides tab, under Master Pages, check **Two-page master**	To create a publication with facing pages. Under Margin Guides, the Left and Right boxes change to Inside and Outside, to reflect the new layout.
4 Set the Top and Bottom margin guides to **6pi**	

Margin Guides

Inside:	3pi
Outside:	3pi
Top:	6pi
Bottom:	6pi

Click **OK**	
5 In the Page Background group, click Master Pages and choose **Edit Master Pages**	The master page is designated as A, and the margins reflect the guide settings you created for the publication.
Click **Close Master Page**	
6 Save the publication as **My newsletter 1**	In the current topic folder.

Insert pages

Explanation

You can insert pages in a publication as necessary by using the Insert Page dialog box, shown in Exhibit 3-2. To do so:

1   On the Insert tab, in the Pages group, click Page and choose Insert Page to open the Insert Page dialog box.

2   In the Number of new pages box, enter the number of pages you want to insert.

3   Select an option for where to insert the new pages:

- Select Before current page to insert the new pages immediately before the current page. (If you're viewing a two-page spread, this option will be Before left page.)

- Select After current page to insert the new pages immediately after the current page. (If you're viewing a two-page spread, this option will be After right page.)

- If you're viewing a two-page spread, you can select Between pages to insert the new pages between the current spread—in effect, splitting the spread at the gutter and inserting new pages.

4   Under Options, choose whether you want to insert a blank page, a page with a text box (which fills the page margins), or a duplicate of an existing page.

5   Click OK.

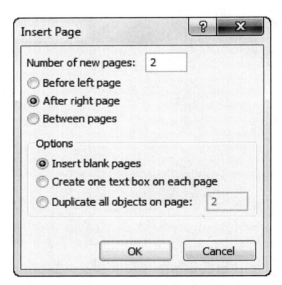

Exhibit 3-2: The Insert Page dialog box

To quickly insert a single page after the current page, you can press Ctrl+Shift+N or, in the Pages group on the Insert tab, click the Insert Blank Page button. If you insert an odd number of pages, Publisher might convert some of the publication's right-facing pages to left-facing pages, and vice versa. This is because the first page is always a single page, rather than a spread.

For example, say you're viewing the page 2–3 spread of a publication, and you want to add a single page before the spread. When you do, the page you insert becomes page 2 (a left-facing page, because even-numbered pages are always left-facing), and the previous page 2 becomes page 3 (a right-facing page). The previous page 3 would now become page 4, a left-facing page on a different spread.

Page icons

In the Page Navigation pane, Publisher displays icons of the pages in your publication. You can use the Page Navigation pane to navigate to a page or spread by clicking it, and you can also rearrange pages and spreads by dragging them in the Page Navigation pane:

- When viewing single pages, drag any page above or below another page.
- When viewing a two-page spread, drag any spread to move it before or after another spread or page. (Moving the spread before the first page will adjust the layout, as discussed above.)
- When viewing a two-page spread, drag any spread as shown in Exhibit 3-3 to move it between the pages of an existing spread. (Again, note that the layout will change as discussed above.)

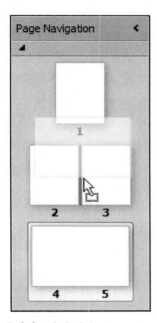

Exhibit 3-3: Moving a two-page spread between the pages of another spread

Do it!

A-2:   Inserting pages in a publication

Here's how	Here's why
1 Click the **Insert** tab	
In the Pages group, click **Page** and choose **Insert Page...**	To open the Insert Page dialog box.
2 Edit the Number of new pages box to read **5**	
Review the options shown in the dialog box	Number of new pages: 5 ○ Before current page ◉ After current page Options ◉ Insert blank pages ○ Create one text box on each page ○ Duplicate all objects on page: 1
	The current options will insert five blank pages after the current page.
Click **OK**	To insert the pages. Publisher moves to page 2.
3 Click the **View** tab	
In the Layout group, click **Two-Page Spread**	To view the publication as a facing-pages layout.
4 In the Page Navigation pane, click the page 1 icon	
	To view the first page of the publication.
5 Update the publication	

Move objects between publications

Explanation

As you develop a publication, you'll likely need to move items, such as stories, headlines, or advertisements, from one page to another, or even from one publication to another. To move objects from one publication to another:

1 Select the objects that you want to move.

2 Press Ctrl+C to place the selected objects on the Clipboard.

3 Open the new publication and navigate to the page on which you want to insert the objects.

4 Press Ctrl+V to paste the objects.

You might need to reposition objects that you paste.

Grouping objects

When you have multiple objects that should always be treated as a unit, you might want to make them a group. Grouping objects makes it easier to scale, rotate, and resize objects that should be treated as a unit. To group objects, select all the objects you want to include in the group (press Shift and click each item); then, on the Home tab, in the Arrange group, click Group. A border appears around all the objects, indicating that they are grouped. When you select one of the grouped objects, all the objects are selected because they act as one unit. To ungroup objects, select them and, in the Arrange group, click Ungroup.

Do it!

A-3: Moving objects between publications

The files for this activity are in Student Data folder **Unit 3\Topic A**.

Here's how	Here's why
1 Open Recipe layout 3	This is a single-page layout that you want to use in a newsletter spread.
2 Press ⌨CTRL + ⌨A	To select all the objects on the page.
3 On the Home tab, in the Arrange group, click **Group**	Grouping objects helps, for example, to ensure that none of the selected objects are accidentally deselected.
4 Press ⌨CTRL + ⌨C	To copy the grouped items to the Clipboard.
5 Click the **View** tab	
In the Window group, click **Switch Windows** and choose **My newsletter 1**	
6 Move to the page 2–3 spread	Click the page 2–3 spread icon in the Page Navigation pane.
7 Press ⌨CTRL + ⌨V	To paste the objects from the Clipboard.
8 Point to the boundary of the heading's text box	**Spicy Buzzard**
	Until the pointer changes to the Move pointer.
Press ⌨SHIFT and drag the grouped objects left	To align them with the page 2 margins. Guides appear when the text box aligns with the margins.
9 Update and close the publication	
10 In the Recipe layout 3 publication, press ⌨CTRL + ⌨W	To close the publication. A warning box appears, asking if you'd like to save the publication.
Click **Don't Save**	

Topic B: Master pages

Explanation

Most publications have some features that are common to all pages. For example, magazines usually have the title and page number on every page. A *master page* acts as a template for pages within a publication. Any items on a master page will automatically be added to pages in a publication to which the master page is applied. Master pages can be single-sided or double-sided.

Working with master pages

Each new publication is created with a default master page designated Master Page A. It contains any margin and column settings you've specified for the publication in the Layout Guides dialog box. To change the guides on the default master page, or to add items to it, click the Page Design tab and, in the Page Background group, click Master Pages and choose Edit Master Pages or press Ctrl+M to view master pages. (You can also click Master Page in the Views group on the View tab.)

To change margin guides or add columns to a master page, first select that master page in the Page Navigation pane. Then, on the Page Design tab, in the Page Setup group, click Margins and choose Custom Margins to open the Layout Guides dialog box. You can then edit the Margin Guides settings. On the Grid Guides tab, shown in Exhibit 3-4, you can also edit the Column Guides and Row Guides boxes to create columns and rows on a page.

Column guides divide pages into vertical sections so you can create evenly spaced columns of text, as in a newspaper or magazine layout. If you specify more than one column, you can also set the space between columns by editing the Spacing box. The space between columns on a layout is also referred to as the *gutter*.

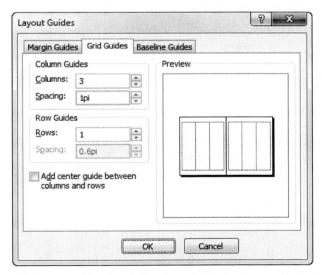

Exhibit 3-4: The Grid Guides tab in the Layout Guides dialog box

Do it!

B-1: Editing the default master page

The files for this activity are in Student Data folder **Unit 3\Topic B**.

Here's how	Here's why
1 Open Newsletter 2	
Save the publication as **My newsletter 2**	
2 On the View tab, in the Views group, click **Master Page**	The Edit Master Pages pane and the Edit Master pages toolbar appear. Master Page A is currently the only master page in the publication.
3 Click the **Page Design** tab	
In the Page Setup group, click **Margins** and select **Custom Margins...**	To open the Layout Guides dialog box.
Click the **Grid Guides** tab	
4 Under Column Guides, edit the Columns box to read **3**	
Press (TAB)	
5 Edit the Spacing box to read **1**	To set the column spacing to 1 pica.
6 Click the **Margin Guides** tab	
7 Set the Top and Bottom margin guides to **3pi**	
Click **OK**	To apply the new guide settings. These guides can help you to align objects precisely into three columns.
8 On the Master Page tab, in the close group, click **Close Master Page**	To return to the publication pages. The publication pages now contain the new margin and column guides.
9 Update the publication	

Creating new master pages

Explanation

If your publication contains several different layouts, then having several different master pages can save you time—after you create more than one master, you can choose which master applies to which pages. To create a new master page:

1 View Master Pages (press Ctrl+M).
2 On the Master Page tab, in the Master Page group, click Add Master Page to open the New Master Page dialog box, shown in Exhibit 3-5.
3 To create a master spread, verify that Two-page master is checked.
4 If desired, edit the Page ID box to use a different, one-character identifier for the master page.
5 If desired, edit the Description box to give the master page a more descriptive title.
6 Click OK.

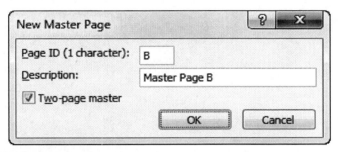

Exhibit 3-5: The New Master Page dialog box

Page numbering

To insert page numbers on master pages that update automatically, click the Insert tab. Then, in the Header & Footer group, click Page Number and select the desired option from the gallery.

To hold the page numbers, Publisher creates text boxes either above or below your current page margins. The character in the text boxes generates the current page number in the layout. All pages based on the master page will display the page number. If you add, delete, or rearrange pages, they're renumbered automatically.

Do it!

B-2: Creating a new master page

The files for this activity are in Student Data folder **Unit 3\Topic B**.

Here's how	Here's why
1 View the master page	(On the View tab, in the View group, click Master Page, or press Ctrl+M.) You'll create a new master page that uses different layout settings.
2 In the Master Page group, click **Add Master Page**	To open the New Master Page dialog box.
Verify that Two-page master is checked	
Click **OK**	To create the new master page. "B" appears in the Page Navigation pane and is selected.
3 On the Page Design tab, in the Page Setup group, click **Margins** and choose **Custom Margins...**	To open the Layout Guides dialog box for Master Page B.
4 Set the Top and Bottom margins to **6pi**	
5 Click the **Grid Guides** tab	
Set the number of columns to **2** and the column spacing to **1pi**	
Click **OK**	
6 Drag a horizontal guide to the 4.5 pica mark on the vertical ruler	(Near the top of the page.) To create a horizontal guide that spans both pages on the master page. Next, you'll add left and right banners to each of the pages.
7 On the Insert tab, in the Illustrations group, click **Picture**	To open the Insert Picture dialog box.
Insert **Left banner**	From the current topic folder.
8 On the left page, move the picture frame so that it snaps between the left and right margins, as shown	Above the new guide.

9 Insert **Right banner** and
position it on the right page, as
shown

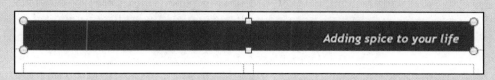

Adding spice to your life

10 Click the **Insert** tab

To open the Page Numbers dialog box. You'll
include automatic page numbers on every page
except the front and back pages.

In the Header & Footer dialog
box, click **Page Number** and
select **Bottom Right**

Publisher creates a footer that aligns with the
inside and outside page margins, below the
bottom margin. A # sign in each text frame
indicates where the page number will appear.

11 Press CTRL + M

To return to page 1 of the publication.

12 Update the publication

Apply master pages

Explanation

After you create or edit a master page and close the master view, you can see which pages use which master pages. To do so, select the page or spread and, on the Page Design tab, in the Page Background group, click Master Pages; the gallery displays the master pages you've created and highlights the one applied to the current pages. To apply a different master to a page or spread, select it from the Master Pages gallery.

When you insert a new page, you can select which master you want to apply to it. To do so, select a master from the Master page list in the Insert Page dialog box, as shown in Exhibit 3-6.

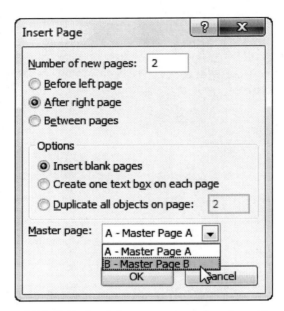

Exhibit 3-6: Applying a master when inserting a new page

Do it!

B-3:   Applying master pages

Here's how	Here's why
1 Go to the page 2–3 spread	Click the spread's icon in the Page Navigation pane.
2 Click the **Page Design** tab	
In the Page Background group, click **Master Pages** and view the gallery	

Pages 2 and 3 have Master Page A applied.

From the Master Pages gallery, select **Master Page B (B)**	To apply Master Page B to pages 2 and 3.
3 Observe the spread	The formatting you applied to the master page is applied to pages 2 and 3.
4 Go to the page 4–5 spread	
5 In the Page Background group, click **Master Pages** and select **Master Page B (B)**	To apply Master Page B.
6 Update and close the publication	

Unit summary: Multi-page publications

Topic A   In this topic, you learned about multi-page layouts. You learned that a **facing-pages layout** is also called a **spread**. You created a facing-pages publication, set **margin guides**, inserted new pages into a publication, and moved items between publications.

Topic B   In this topic, you learned how to work with **master pages**. You learned how to edit default master pages, set **column guides**, and create new master pages. You also **inserted images** onto a master spread. Finally, you set automatic **page numbering**, and you **applied master pages** to the pages of a publication.

Independent practice activity

In this activity, you'll create a facing-pages publication and copy items to it from another publication. Then you'll create and edit master pages, and insert images and page numbers.

The files for this activity are in Student Data folder **Unit 3\Unit summary**.

1 Open Note 2.

2 Create a new facing-pages publication titled **My spreads**. (*Hint*: In the Layout Guides dialog box, check **Two-page master**.)

3 Set the margins using the following values: inside and outside margins of **3pi**, top margin of **12pi**, bottom margin of **6pi**.

4 Insert two new pages after the current page.

5 View the pages as a two-page spread.

6 Copy the items from the Note 2 publication to page 2 of the My spreads publication. Then close Note 2. (*Hint*: If a dialog box appears asking if you'd like to save the Clipboard, click No.)

7 Create a new master spread (i.e., Master Page B) for the My spreads publication. Set the margin guides using the following values: inside and outside margins of **6pi**, top margin of **12pi**, bottom margin of **3pi**.

8 Insert the Left bar and Right bar images. Position them as shown in Exhibit 3-7.

9 Add page numbers to both the left and right master pages, positioned at the top-right of the layout pages.

10 View pages 2 and 3 in the publication. Apply Master Page B to the page 2-3 spread.

11 Adjust the objects so that the two pages look similar to the pages shown in Exhibit 3-8. (*Hint*: Select all the items on the page, and then align the heading to fit within the margins.)

12 Update and close the publication.

Exhibit 3-7: The new master pages after step 8

Exhibit 3-8: Pages 2 and 3 after step 11

Review questions

1 A publication that contains spreads has what kinds of pages?

A Extra-wide pages

B Pages with a landscape orientation

C Pages that fold out like an accordion

D Left- and right-facing pages

2 You want to insert one new page between an existing spread. How will this affect the publication's existing pages?

3 In a publication, you want some pages to use a three-column layout and others to use a two-column layout. How can you easily apply this formatting to new or existing pages?

A Copy and paste the column formatting.

B Use a template.

C Specify the column guides for each page.

D Create master pages.

4 You've inserted page numbers on a master page, which you've applied to the publication. However, now you want to add some new pages and delete some existing pages. How can you update the page numbering?

5 In a facing-pages layout, page 1 appears with page 2 in a spread. True or false?

Unit 4

Working with text

Unit time: 60 minutes

Complete this unit, and you'll know how to:

A Link and unlink text boxes and add continuation notices.

B Set tab stops, format paragraphs, control indents and spacing, and create drop caps.

Topic A: Text box linking

Explanation   Multiple-page publications often contain one or more stories that begin in one text box and continue into other text boxes on the same page, or on other pages. You can use Publisher to control how text flows between text boxes.

Controlling text flow

You can link text boxes so that the text from one text box flows into another text box, either on the same page or on a different page. For example, some layouts consist of multiple columns of text. Content in the text box in the first column typically continues to the text box at the top of the next column.

Newsletters, magazines, and newspapers often try to place as many stories as possible on the front page, and then continue the stories on subsequent pages. You can link text boxes on different pages so that a story beginning on page 1 can continue seamlessly on another page. If you add text to the first text box, the text flows into the linked text box.

To link text boxes:

1   Select the first text box.

2   Click the Text Box Tools | Format tab.

3   In the Linking group, click Create Link.

4   Click an empty text box to create the link. (You can also click an empty area of the layout to create a new text box.) If the first text box contains more text than it can contain, the text will flow from the first box to the next.

5   Link additional text boxes as necessary by repeating steps 1 through 4.

When a selected text box contains text that links to a previous text box, an icon appears at the top-left of the text box. Click it to go to the previous text box. Likewise, when a selected text box contains text that continues in another linked text box, an icon appears at the bottom-right of the text box.

When you insert text that doesn't fit into an existing text box, Publisher automatically creates a new text box on the next blank page; if a blank page doesn't exist, then Publisher creates one.

Do it!   **A-1:   Linking text boxes**

The files for this activity are in Student Data folder **Unit 4\Topic A**.

Here's how	Here's why
1 Open Newsletter 3	
Save the publication as **My newsletter 3**	In the current topic folder.
2 On page 1, create a text box in the center column, as shown	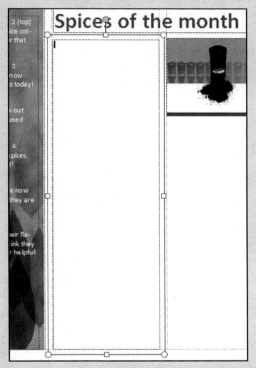

You want to insert a long story that won't fit in this text box, so you'll create another text box and link them.

3 Create a text box in the right column, as shown	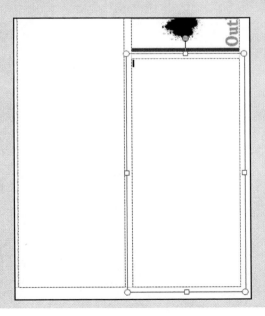

4 Click the text box in the center column	To select it.
5 On Text Box Tools | Format tab, in the Linking group, click **Create Link**	
Point to the text box in the right column	
	The pointer changes to indicate any text overflowing the selected text box will "pour" into the text box you're pointing to.
Click the right column	To link the text box. An icon appears, indicating that the text box is linked to another text box.
	You'll link these text boxes to another one, so that the story can "jump" from the first page to another page in the newsletter.
6 In the Linking group, click **Create Link**	
Go to page 2	
Click in the left column, as shown	
	To create a new text box linked to the previous one.
7 Go to page 1	
8 Place the insertion point in the first text box	In the center column.
9 On the Insert tab, in the Text group, click **Insert File**	To open the Insert Text dialog box.
Select **Spices of the month**	In the current topic folder.
Click **OK**	The text flowed from the first text box to the second, and then to the third text box, on page 2. However, there was more text than could fit in these boxes, so Publisher created a new text box on the first empty page, page 6.
10 Update the publication	

Breaking text box links

Explanation

When you link text boxes across pages, you might need to modify the flow of text by breaking some links and creating new ones. To break a text box link, select the text box containing a forward link. Then, on the Text Box Tools | Format tab, in the Linking group, click Break to break the link between the selected text box and all ones that come after it in the series. You then can link the text box to another text box. You can also break a link by deleting a text box—text will flow into the next text box in the series, if one is available. By using this method, you can break a link to a single text box in a series without severing the link between previous text boxes and ones that come next.

Do it!

A-2:   Breaking a text box link

Here's how	Here's why
1 On page 3, create a text box in the left column, as shown	
2 On page 1, click the text box in the right column	The second text box in the series.
On the Text Box Tools	Format tab, in the Linking group, click **Break**	To break the link between this text box and all text boxes that come after it in the series.
3 In the Linking group, click **Create Link**	
4 On page 3, click the empty text box you created	To link it. The text overflows this text box.
At the bottom-right of the text box, click as show	To load the overflow text.
Click in the right column	To place the overflow text in a new text box.
5 Update the publication	

Continuation notices

Explanation

When you link text from one page to another page, continuation notices help your readers to know where the text continues and originates from. Examples of "continued on" and "continued from" notices are shown in Exhibit 4-1.

To add continuation notices:

1   Right-click a text box that has a forward link to another text box and choose Format Text Box to open the Format Text Box dialog box.

2   Click the Text Box tab.

3   At the bottom of the dialog box, check Include "Continued on page…".

4   Click OK.

5   Go to the page containing the text box with the continued text. Right-click the text box containing the link to a previous text box and choose Format Text Box.

6   On the Text Box tab of the Format Text Box dialog box, check Include "Continued from page…" and click OK.

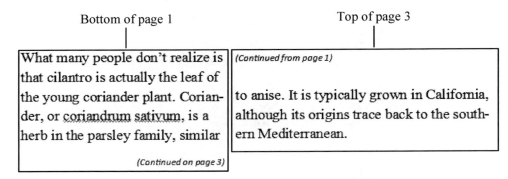

Exhibit 4-1: Continuation notices indicating that text flows from page 1 to page 3

Do it!

A-3: Adding continuation notices

Here's how	Here's why
1 Go to page 1	You'll create a continuation notice at the bottom of the right column that tells readers where the article continues.
2 Zoom in on the bottom-right corner of the page	Right-click and choose Zoom, 150%; then scroll to the bottom-right corner.
3 Right-click in the text box in the right column and choose **Format Text Box...**	To open the Format Text Box dialog box.
4 Click the **Text Box** tab	
Check **Include "Continued on page..."**	
Click **OK**	To insert a continuation notice at the bottom of the text. The text automatically appears, indicating the correct continuation page.
5 Go to page 3	
6 Right-click the text box in the left column and choose **Format Text Box...**	
7 Click the **Text Box** tab	
Check **Include "Continued from page..."**	
Click **OK**	To insert a continued-from notice at the top of the text.
8 Update and close the publication	

Topic B: Paragraph formatting

Explanation

Formatting that you apply to entire paragraphs is commonly referred to as paragraph formatting. Line spacing, indents, and keep settings are a few examples of formatting options that affect entire paragraphs.

Aligning text with tabs

Tab stops allow you to align text horizontally within single lines or paragraphs. Exhibit 4-2 shows the tab alignments available in Publisher. When setting tab stops, you can specify a *leader*, which is a series of dots, dashes, lines, or bullets preceding a tab stop. It's often easiest to press Tab to insert tab characters prior to setting tab alignments or leaders, so that you can see the results of the tab settings as you set them.

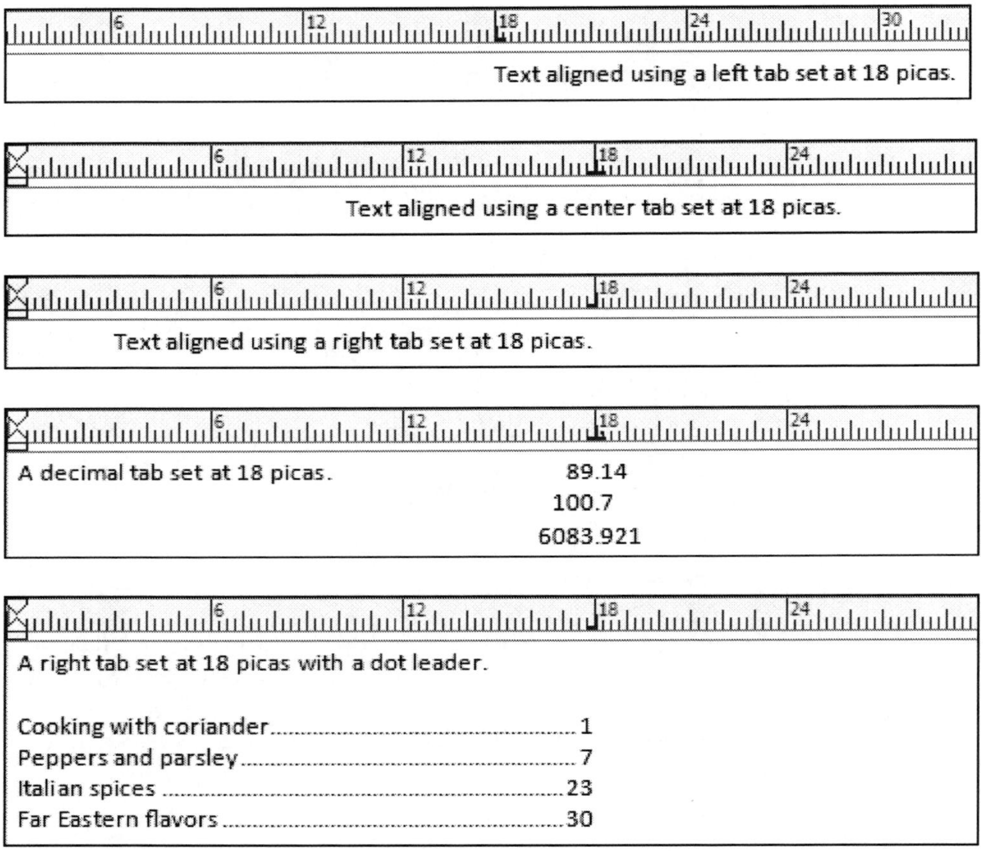

Text aligned using a left tab set at 18 picas.

Text aligned using a center tab set at 18 picas.

Text aligned using a right tab set at 18 picas.

A decimal tab set at 18 picas.
89.14
100.7
6083.921

A right tab set at 18 picas with a dot leader.

Cooking with coriander...1
Peppers and parsley..7
Italian spices 23
Far Eastern flavors 30

Exhibit 4-2: Available tab formatting options

To set, clear, or modify a tab stop:

1　Select the paragraph(s) containing the text with tabs (or the paragraph to which you'll add tab characters).

2　On the Home tab, click the Paragraph group dialog box launcher to open the Paragraph dialog box, shown in Exhibit 4-3. Click the Tabs tab.

3　In the Tab stop position box, enter the position on the horizontal ruler where you want to create a tab stop. (Default tab stops are every 3 picas.)

4　Under Alignment, select the desired tab type.

5　If desired, select a leader for the tab stop.

6　Click Set to add the tab stop to the Tab stop position list.

7　Create additional tab stops as desired. (Remember to click Set after specifying the desired options.)

8　When you're finished adding, modifying, or clearing tab stops, click OK.

To change a tab stop's alignment or leader, select the tab stop in the Paragraph dialog box, select the desired options, and then click Set. To remove a tab stop, select the tab stop in the Paragraph dialog box and click Clear.

You can also set tab stops by selecting a paragraph and then clicking the horizontal ruler. The default tab stop is left tab. To change the tab type, click the tab stop icon at the intersection of the two rulers—you'll cycle through left, center, right, and decimal tabs. To remove a tab, drag the tab stop indicator from the tab ruler and release the mouse button.

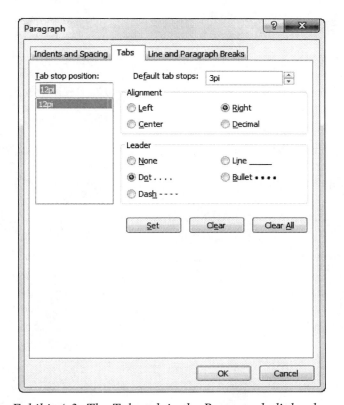

Exhibit 4-3: The Tabs tab in the Paragraph dialog box

Do it!

B-1: Setting tab stops and creating a leader

The files for this activity are in Student Data folder **Unit 4\Topic B**.

Here's how	Here's why
1 Open Newsletter 4	
Save the publication as **My newsletter 4**	In the current topic folder.
2 On page 1, select the left text box containing the list of articles	Zoom in, if necessary.
Press `CTRL` + `A`	To select all the text in this text box.
3 On the Home tab, in the Paragraph group, click the dialog box launcher, as indicated	To open the Paragraph dialog box.
4 Click the **Tabs** tab	You'll set a left tab at 9.75 picas so that the page numbers align with the right side of the text box.
In the Tab stop position box, type **9.75**	A left tab with no leader is selected by default.
Click **Set**	
Click **OK**	To create a left tab.
5 Change the font size to 10 points	So that the text on the top line of each entry doesn't wrap to the next line. You'll change the tab setting to a right tab with a dot leader.
6 Open the Paragraph dialog box	(Click the Paragraph dialog box launcher.)
Click the **Tabs** tab	Because you've entered only one tab stop, it's selected by default.
Click **Clear**	To clear the existing tab stop.
7 In the Tab stop position box, enter **12**	
Under Alignment, select **Right**	
Under Leader, Select **Dot**	
Click **Set**	
Click **OK**	To close the dialog box. Now, the space between each entry and its corresponding page number has a dotted leader.
8 Update the publication	

Indents

Explanation

You might find that text is too close to the edges of a text box, page margin, or column. You can use indents to move the text away from those edges in order to improve readability.

You can also create a first line indent, which is a common technique in publishing. In this type of indent, the first line of a paragraph is offset from the edge of the text box, which is similar to placing a tab at the beginning of a paragraph.

To add left or right indents to text:

1 Select the paragraph(s) you want to indent.

2 On the Home tab, click the Paragraph group dialog box launcher to open the Paragraph dialog box.

3 On the Indents and Spacing tab, set the desired indents for the text:

- If you want to indent all the text in the selected paragraphs from the left side of the text box, edit the Left box.

- If you want to indent just the first line of text in each selected paragraph, edit the First line box.

- If you want to indent all the text in the selected paragraphs from the right side of the text box, edit the Right box.

- To use a preset indentation, select an option from the Preset list. For example, the preset 1st Line Indent sets the first line indent to 3 picas.

4 Click OK.

Set indents by using the ruler

You might not always know exactly how much you want to indent text. You can set indents visually by dragging the indent marks on the horizontal ruler. To set indents with the ruler, first select the paragraph(s) you want to indent. Then drag the first line, left indent, and right indent markers, shown in Exhibit 4-4, to where you want them on the ruler.

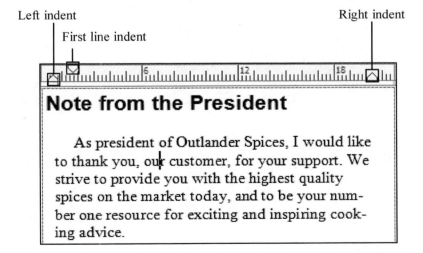

Exhibit 4-4: Setting indents by dragging the indent markers on the ruler

Do it!

B-2: Creating indents

Here's how	Here's why
1 Go to page 5	You'll indent the quotes in the Note from the President article.
Select the two paragraphs shown	Outlander Spices has been great for my restaurant! Our customers love our new recipes and keep coming back. Thanks! – Bob Gardner, Phila., PA I love to cook, but often felt like I was using spices incorrectly. Thanks to your newsletter, I'm always assured the foods I cook taste great! Thanks Outlander Spices! – Jan Salinksy, Dayton, OH Reaching out to every kitchen—that's Outlander Spices!
	The quotes from Outlander customers.
2 On the Home tab, click the Paragraph dialog box launcher	To open the Paragraph dialog box.
3 Verify that the Indents and Spacing tab is activated	
Edit the Left box to read **1**	
Edit the Right box to read **1**	
Click **OK**	To create a block indent of 1 pica. Next, you'll indent just the first line of these paragraphs.
4 Open the Paragraph dialog box	Click the Paragraph dialog box launcher.
Edit the First line box to read **1**	
Click **OK**	To set the first line indent to 1 pica for the selected paragraphs.
5 Press (CTRL) + (I)	To italicize the selected text.
6 Update the publication	

Bulleted lists

Explanation

Bulleted or numbered lists typically appear with a hanging indent, in which the bullet or number appears to the left of any subsequent lines of text in the paragraph, as shown in the first bullet in Exhibit 4-5. You can create a bulleted list from a selected paragraph by clicking the Bullets button in the Paragraph group, on the Home tab, and selecting an option from the gallery.

Method

- Preheat oven to 425 degrees.
- In a bowl, mix paprika, caraway seeds, onion flakes, dry mustard, thyme leaves, salt, and ground red pepper.
- With hands, lightly pat paprika mixture on chicken wings.
- Brush chicken wings with Buzzard's Best Hot Wing Sauce.
- Place chicken wings in a large baking dish.
- Bake 30 minutes or until chicken wings are fork-tender.
- Place chicken wings on platter. Garnish with celery.

Exhibit 4-5: A bulleted list that uses hanging indents

When you select an option from the Bullets gallery, Publisher converts the selected paragraphs to a bulleted list, using default options. To format a bulleted list, select it; then click the Bullets button and choose Bullets and Numbering to open the Bullets and Numbering dialog box, shown in Exhibit 4-6. From the Bullets and Numbering dialog box, you can select a different bullet character, adjust the size of the bullet character, and adjust the distance the text is indented from the bullet character.

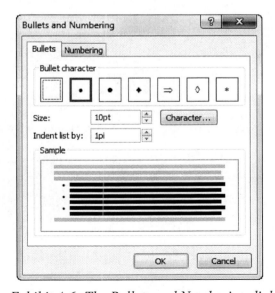

Exhibit 4-6: The Bullets and Numbering dialog box

B-3: Creating a bulleted list

Here's how	Here's why
1 Go to page 4	
2 Select the indicated paragraphs	Method Preheat oven to 425 degrees. In a bowl mix paprika, caraway seeds, onion flakes, dry mustard, thyme leaves, salt, and ground red pepper. With hands, lightly pat paprika mixture on chicken wings. Brush chicken wings with Buzzard's Best Hot Wing Sauce. Place chicken wings in a large baking dish. Bake 30 minutes or until chicken wings are fork-tender. Place chicken wings on platter. Garnish with celery.
On the Home tab, in the Paragraph dialog box, click	(The Bullets button.) To display the Bullets gallery.
Select the indicated option	**Bullet Styles** None Small Bullets. To format the paragraphs as bullets. Next, you'll adjust the bullet formatting.
3 Click the Bullets button and choose **Bullets and Numbering...**	To open the Bullets and Numbering dialog box.
Edit the Indent list by box to read **1**	To indent the text after the bullet by 1 pica.
Click **OK**	To close the dialog box.
4 Open the Paragraph dialog box	Click the Paragraph dialog box launcher.
5 Set the left indent to **2**	To indent the bulleted paragraphs by 2 picas.
Click **OK**	To close the dialog box.
6 Update the publication	

Keep settings

Explanation

In multi-page or multi-column publications, it's important to prevent widows and orphans. A *widow* occurs when the first line in a paragraph is left as the last line of a column or page, while the paragraph's remaining lines appear in the following column or page. An *orphan* is the last line in a paragraph displayed as the first line of a column or page, while all of the preceding lines of the paragraph are in the previous column or page. Exhibit 4-7 shows an example of a widow.

Exhibit 4-7: An example of a widow

You should also ensure that a heading or subheading appears with at least a portion of the paragraph it serves. Otherwise, it won't be clear to the reader that it's a heading, and the reader might not implicitly associate it with the corresponding text. You can specify keep settings to control widows and orphans and to keep headings or subheadings with their corresponding text. To do so, use the keep settings on the Line and Page Breaks tab of the Paragraph dialog box. The following table describes the various keep settings.

Keep setting	Description
Widow/Orphan control	Prevents a paragraph from producing widows or orphans when breaking across columns or pages.
Keep with next	Forces the selected paragraph to stay in the same column or page as the paragraph that follows.
Keep lines together	Forces all the lines in the selected paragraph to stay together, preventing the paragraph from breaking at all across columns or pages.
Start in new text box	Forces the selected paragraph to begin in a new text box. If a text box isn't already linked, you'll have to create a new one and flow the text into it.

Do it!

B-4:   Applying a keep setting

Here's how	Here's why
1 Go to page 2	
2 Verify that all the text for the Outlander Spice Collection article is visible	Zoom as necessary to view the text of both columns in the document window. Notice that there's a widow in the left column.
3 Observe the last line of text in the left column	This is an example of a widow—for better readability and continuity, it belongs at the top of the next paragraph.
Click anywhere in the paragraph at the top of the right column	
4 Open the Paragraph dialog box	
Click the **Line and Paragraph Breaks** tab	
Check **Widow/Orphan control**	
Click **OK**	The widowed line moves to the top of the right text box.
5 Update the publication	

Vertical spacing

Explanation

Adjusting vertical spacing between lines of text in a paragraph, and between paragraphs, can make the text in a document more readable and engaging. In the Paragraph dialog box, you can set spacing between lines of a paragraph, before paragraphs, and after paragraphs.

Single spacing means there's no space before or after lines in a paragraph. In the Paragraph dialog box, this is equivalent to 1sp. Publisher 2010's default paragraph spacing, however, is slightly more—1.19sp. This means that lines of text are spaced a bit farther apart than you might be used to, so you might want to adjust this setting in the Paragraph dialog box if you're accustomed to using single spacing. However, increased spacing between lines can often make text easier to read. Exhibit 4-8 shows body text using the default 1.19sp setting, compared to the same text using 1sp spacing.

Note from the President

As president of Outlander Spices, I would like to thank you, our customer, for your support. We strive to provide you with the highest quality spices on the market today, and to be your number one resource for exciting and inspiring cooking advice.

Note from the President

As president of Outlander Spices, I would like to thank you, our customer, for your support. We strive to provide you with the highest quality spices on the market today, and to be your number one resource for exciting and inspiring cooking advice.

Exhibit 4-8: Paragraphs using Publisher's default (left) and single spacing (right)

You can set the spacing between lines to a relative value, such as 1sp, to maintain the same relative spacing between lines, even if, for example, you adjust the type size. You can also set line spacing by using precise values. For example, you could set a paragraph to use 18-point spacing. However, if you change the type size in a paragraph that uses a fixed value for line spacing, the spacing will still be 18 points, so lines of text might overlap or appear too far apart.

To set the space between lines, open the Paragraph dialog box and edit the value in the Between lines box. You can also select some preset options from the Line Spacing menu, in the Paragraph group on the Home tab.

Paragraph Spacing

You can also customize the space between paragraphs. Instead of adding an extra return character between paragraphs, you can set specific space values between paragraphs. Publisher 2010 specifies a default spacing of 6pt after paragraphs.

To create vertical space between paragraphs:

1   Select the paragraphs to which you want to apply paragraph spacing.
2   Open the Paragraph dialog box.
3   Under Line spacing, specify values in the Before paragraphs or After paragraphs boxes.
4   Click OK.

You can also select some preset options from the Paragraph Spacing menu, in the Paragraph group on the Home tab.

Do it!

B-5:   Adjusting vertical spacing

Here's how	Here's why
1 Go to page 5	You'll adjust the spacing between each paragraph in the Note from the President article.
2 On the Home tab, in the Paragraph group, click ¶	(The Special Characters button.) To view the formatting characters, which can help you to work more precisely with text. The paragraphs are currently spaced using extra paragraph returns, which is not the best way to control spacing.

3 Delete the extra paragraph returns between paragraphs

> **Note·from·the·President¶**
> As·president·of·Outlander·Spices,·I·would·like·to·thank·you,·our·customer,·for·your·support.·We·strive·to·provide·you·with·the·highest·quality·spices·on·the·market·today,·and·to·be·your·number·one·resource·for·exciting·and·inspiring·cooking·advice.¶
> With·our·new·website·and·publications·such·as·this·newsletter,·we·offer·helpful·recipes,·cooking·tips,·and·cooking·products·to·make·preparing·food·a·much·more·fulfilling·experience.·We·know·we're·making·a·difference·based·on·the·positive·feedback·we've·received!¶
> *Outlander·Spices·has·been·great·for·my·restaurant!·Our·customers·love·our·new·recipes·and·keep·coming·back.·Thanks!·—·Bob·Gardner,·Phila.,·PA¶*
> *I·love·to·cook,·but·often·felt·like·I·was·using·spices·incorrectly.·Thanks·to·your·newsletter,·I'm·always·assured·the·foods·I·cook·taste·great!·Thanks·Outlander·Spices!·—·Jan·Salinsky,·Dayton,·OH¶*
> Reaching·out·to·every·kitchen—that's·Outlander·Spices!¤

4 Select all the text in the text box

Click anywhere in the text and press Ctrl+A.

5 On the Home tab, in the Paragraph group, click ≡ ▾

(The Paragraph Spacing button.) To view the Paragraph Spacing menu.

From the Line Spacing menu, choose **Paragraph Spacing Options...**

To open the Paragraph dialog box.

Under Line spacing, edit the After paragraphs box to read **6pt**

This is the default used in Publisher 2010 for new and inserted text.

Click **OK**

6 points of spacing is added after each paragraph.

6 Deselect the text

To view the paragraph spacing more clearly.

7 Under the heading, select all the body text

Do not select the heading.

8 On the Home tab, in the Paragraph group, click ⬍≡ ▾

(The Line Spacing button.) To view the Line Spacing menu.

Choose **1.5**

To increase the spacing to 1.5sp.

The text overflows the text box.

9 On the Text Box Tools | Format tab, in the Text group, click **Text Fit** and choose **Grow Text Box to Fit**

To automatically resize the text box to fit the text within it. Publisher adjusts the bottom boundary of the text box.

10 Hide the special characters

Click the Special Characters button, on the Home tab.

11 Update the publication

Drop caps

Explanation

Drop caps are stylistic typographic elements, typically an oversized initial letter, which extend down into a paragraph by two or more lines. In Publisher, they are measured by the number of lines they overlap. For example, a drop cap with a setting of 3 extends down into the first three lines in a paragraph, as shown in Exhibit 4-9.

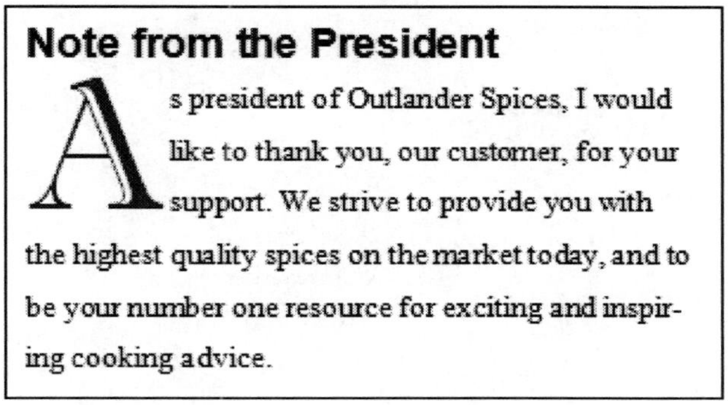

Exhibit 4-9: A drop cap

You can choose from several pre-defined drop cap styles in the Drop Cap gallery, on the Text Box Tools | Format tab, or you can create a custom drop cap. To create a custom drop cap:

1   Place the insertion point in the paragraph.

2   On the Text Box Tools | Format tab, in the Typography group, click Drop Cap and choose Custom Drop Cap to open the Drop Cap dialog box, shown in Exhibit 4-10.

3   Select the letter position and size.

4   Edit the Size of letters box to specify the number of lines the character is dropped in the paragraph.

5   Edit the Number of letters box to specify the number of characters included in the drop cap. Use the Preview window to verify your results.

6   Under Select letter appearance, check or clear options to select font, font style, and color options.

7   Click Apply to view the results in the layout, and adjust them if necessary.

8   When the settings are correct, click OK.

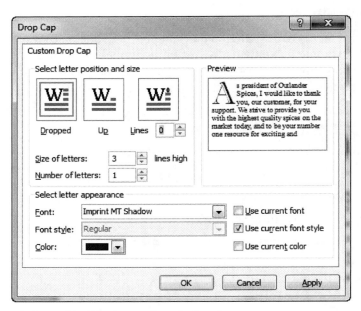

Exhibit 4-10: The Drop Cap dialog box

Do it!

B-6: Creating a drop cap

Here's how	Here's why
1 Click anywhere in the first paragraph beneath the heading	(In the "Note from the President" article.) You'll make the first letter in the word "As" a drop cap.
2 On the Text Box Tools | Format tab, in the Typography group, click **Drop Cap**	To view the Drop Cap gallery.
Select the indicated option	Drop Cap Style 6.
3 In the Typography group, click **Drop Cap** and choose **Custom Drop Cap...**	
Edit the Size of letters box to read **3**	
Verify that the Number of letters box is set to **1**	
Click **OK**	To modify the drop cap.
4 Update and close the publication	

Unit summary: Working with text

Topic A   In this topic, you learned how to **link text boxes** to establish content flow across pages, **break text box links**, and create **continuation notices**.

Topic B   In this topic, you learned how to create **tab stops** and a **leader**, create and adjust **indents**, apply and format **bullets**, set **keep settings** to prevent common typesetting errors such as widows and orphans, control **vertical spacing** and **paragraph spacing**, and create **drop caps**.

Independent practice activity

In this activity, you'll link text boxes so that text flows between them. Then you'll adjust the paragraph formatting.

The files for this activity are in Student Data folder **Unit 4\Unit summary**.

1 Open **Note 3** and save it as **My note 3**.

2 Go to page 4. The text box in the left column contains more text than it can display. Link the text box to the empty text box in the right column on page 4.

3 Format the text on page 4 so that there's a **12pt** space after each paragraph.

4 The spacing you've set produces a widow at the bottom of the first column. Set the paragraph formatting so that widows and orphans won't appear in this text.

5 Format the paragraph under the heading Introduction to use a drop cap of your choice.

6 Update and close the publication.

Review questions

1 If you want text in a text box on page 1 of a document to continue into a text box on page 3, what do you need to do?

2 When should you use continuation notices?

   A When the story will continue in the next edition.

   B When a story is incomplete.

   C When the text of a story flows from one page to another.

   D When the text of a story doesn't entirely fill a text box.

3 What are the four kinds of alignment that you can apply to a tab stop?

4 Indenting can set the edge of text for the:

   A Left side of the paragraph

   B Right side of the paragraph

   C First line of the paragraph

   D All of the above

5 What's a widow?

6 What's an orphan?

7 An oversized initial letter that begins a paragraph is called a:

   A Bold cap

   B Drop cap

   C Descender

   D Starting cap

Unit 5

Tables

Unit time: 60 minutes

Complete this unit, and you'll know how to:

A Create tables and create a table from imported data.

B Modify a table's structure.

C Format tables and edit an Excel spreadsheet in Publisher.

Topic A: Table basics

Some kinds of information are easier to understand when they are presented in tables. For example, Exhibit 5-1 shows the same financial information presented both as paragraph text and in a table. The paragraph above the table contains the same information, but it's arguably clearer and easier to read when presented as tabular data.

The Basic collection, $39.95, contains 10 common spices plus trays, quick reference, and recipe book. The Deluxe collection, $49.95, contains the Basic set plus your choice of 5 Southwestern or 5 Asian spices. The Complete set, $59.95, contains the Basic set, 5 Southwestern spices, and 5 Asian spices.

Collection	Includes	Price
Basic	10 common spices plus trays, quick reference, and recipe book	$39.95
Deluxe	Basic set plus your choice of 5 Southwestern or 5 Asian spices	$49.95
Complete	Basic set, 5 Southwestern spices, and 5 Asian spices	$59.95

Exhibit 5-1: Data presented as text compared to the same data in a table

Creating tables

Although you can use tabs to manipulate text so that it is aligned in rows and columns, this process can be time-consuming. When you have a lot of text to align into rows and columns, tables are easier to use.

To create a table like the one shown in Exhibit 5-1, you need to first create the table and then either type content into the table cells, or copy and paste content into them.

To insert a table quickly:

1   Place the insertion point where you want the table to go.
2   Click the Home tab. (You can also use the Insert tab.)
3   In the Objects group, click Table to display the Table gallery, shown in Exhibit 5-2.
4   Point to the squares in the gallery to indicate the size of the table you want to create. As you point, the squares are highlighted, and Publisher shows a preview of the table in the document.
5   Click the gallery to insert the table.

When creating a table, you specify the number of rows and columns. The intersection of a row and a column is called a cell.

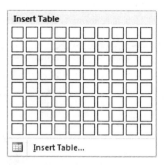

Exhibit 5-2: The Table gallery

Using the Create Table dialog box

In the Objects group on the Home tab, click Table and choose Insert Table to open the Create Table dialog box. Here, you can specify the number of columns and rows the new table should have.

Resizing a table

You can resize a table to fit it within a layout, as needed. You can resize a selected table by dragging any one of the resize handles located on the table's outer edges. When you resize a table, the columns and rows resize proportionally.

Moving between cells

To navigate in a table, you can click in a cell to place the insertion point, or you can use several keys, as described in the following table.

Press this key	To do this
Tab	Move one cell to the right.
Shift+Tab	Move one cell to the left.
Up Arrow	Move up one row.
Down Arrow	Move down one row.

Pressing Tab in a table moves the insertion point to the next cell; therefore, you cannot use Tab to insert a tab character, as you would in a text box. To insert a tab character in a table, press Ctrl+Tab.

A-1: Creating a table

The files for this activity are in Student Data folder **Unit 5\Topic A**.

Here's how	Here's why
1 Open Newsletter 5	
Save the publication as **My newsletter 5**	In the current topic folder.
2 Go to page 2	You'll create a table for the text comparing the three spice sets.
3 Select the text box containing the spice sets information	about improve their culinary concoctions. Order yours today on our website. $39.95 Basic 10 common spices plus trays, quick reference, and recipe book $49.95 Deluxe Basic set plus your choice of 5 Southwestern or 5 Asian spices $59.95 Complete Basic set, 5 Southwestern spices, and 5 Asian spices
Drag the text box into the pasteboard to the left of the page	To temporarily move the content off the page. You'll cut and paste the content into a table.
4 On the Home tab, in the Objects group, click **Table**	To view the Table gallery.
Point to the gallery	As you point to the Table gallery, Publisher highlights squares, which represent table cells. In addition, Publisher begins to draw the table in the publication.
Click as shown	3x4 Table
	To create a table with three rows and four columns.
5 Drag the table to the space formerly occupied by the text box you moved to the pasteboard	about improve their culinary concoctions. Order yours today on our website.

6	Right-click the table and choose **Zoom, Selected Objects**	To zoom in on the table. You'll create a heading in the top row of the table.

7 Verify that the insertion point is in the top left cell

Type **Collection**

In the top-left cell of the table.

8 Press (TAB)

To move the insertion point to the next cell to the right.

Type **Includes**

9 Move the insertion point to the next cell

Press Tab.

Type **Price**

Collection	Includes	Price

To complete the header row.

10 Move to the first cell of the second row

Type **Basic**

11 In the first cell of the third row, **Deluxe**

12 In the first cell of the fourth row, type **Complete**

Right-click and choose **Zoom, Whole Page**

13 Cut and paste the text from the text box you moved to the pasteboard into the table cells, as shown

Collection	Includes	Price
Basic	10 common spices plus trays, quick reference, and recipe book	$39.95
Deluxe	Basic set plus your choice of 5 Southwestern or 5 Asian spices	$49.95
Complete	Basic set, 5 Southwestern spices, and 5 Asian spices	$59.95

By default, text you copy and paste retains its original formatting.

14 Update the publication

Importing Excel data

Explanation

You can insert content from other applications into Publisher and maintain the ability to edit the content in its original application so that it's updated in Publisher. To do this, you must use applications that support Object Linking and Embedding (OLE). When you insert content in this way, the content is referred to as an *object*.

The file you insert into Publisher is referred to as the *source file*. When you insert a source file as an object, it is embedded in the publication by default. An *embedded object* is stored in the publication and is separate from the source file. Changes you make in the source file are not reflected in the embedded version in the publication.

If you want source-file changes to be reflected in the version you inserted into Publisher, you *link* the object rather than embed it. You can then open the source file from within Publisher by double-clicking the linked object.

To generate a table from an Excel file:

1   On the Insert tab, in the Text group, click Object to open the Insert Object dialog box, shown in Exhibit 5-3.

2   Select Create from file.

3   Click Browse to open the Browse dialog box.

4   Select the Excel file that contains the data you want to insert and click Open.

5   If desired, check Link to create a link to the original file. Then, when you edit the original Excel sheet, the data in Publisher will be updated automatically. Otherwise, the content will be embedded.

6   Click OK to generate the table.

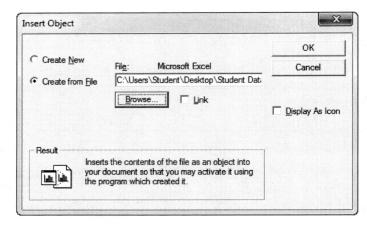

Exhibit 5-3: The Insert Object dialog box

Do it!

A-2: Importing an Excel document

The files for this activity are in Student Data folder **Unit 5\Topic A**.

Here's how	Here's why
1 Go to page 3	
2 Zoom in on the empty space at the bottom of the page	You'll insert an Excel file containing spice information.
3 On the Insert tab, in the Text group, click **Object**	To open the Insert Object dialog box.
Select **Create from File**	
Click **Browse...**	To open the Browse dialog box.
4 Navigate to the current topic folder	
Select **Peppers**	
Click **Open**	To return to the Insert Object dialog box.
5 Click **OK**	To embed the Excel worksheet into the publication. You'll format the data later.
6 Update and close the publication	

Topic B: Table structure

Explanation

You can modify a table's structure in a variety of ways. You can insert and delete rows and columns as needed, you can modify the width and height of cells to accommodate content size, and you can customize the table's appearance.

Rows and columns

You can modify a table by inserting rows and/or columns. You can also delete a row or column or change the width and height of a column or row.

You can add rows and columns to a table by using the options on the Table Tools | Layout tab. You also can right-click a table and access commands in the shortcut menu. The following table lists techniques you can use for adding rows and columns.

To add...	Do this
A row	Place the insertion point in a row. In the Rows & Columns group, click Insert Above or Insert Below; or right-click and choose Insert, Insert Above or Insert Below.
Multiple rows	Select as many rows in the table as you want to insert. In the Rows & Columns group, click Insert Above or Insert Below; or right-click and choose Insert, Insert Above or Insert Below.
A column	Place the insertion point in a column. In the Rows & Columns group, click Insert Right or Insert Left; or right-click and choose Insert, Insert Left or Insert Right.
Multiple columns	Select as many columns in the table as you want to add. In the Rows & Columns group, click Insert Right or Insert Left; or right-click and choose Insert, Insert Left or Insert Right.

You can also add a row to the bottom of a table by placing the insertion point in the last cell of the last row and pressing Tab.

You can delete rows and columns from tables, or delete an entire table, by using commands in the Rows & Columns group or by pressing Backspace. However, you can't delete rows, columns, or tables by pressing Delete. The Delete key deletes only the text in a table, not the table structure itself.

Adjusting row and column dimensions

To adjust the width and height of rows and columns in a table, point to one of the grid lines. When you do, the pointer changes to an icon with two arrows pointing in opposite directions. You can then drag the grid line in either direction to make the row or column wider or narrower.

Do it!

B-1: Modifying table cells

Here's how	Here's why
1 Open Newsletter 6	
Save the publication as **My newsletter 6**	
2 Go to page 5	You'll create a new column in the table at the bottom of the page.
3 Click any table cell	(In the Spice tips table.) There's only one column in the table.
4 On the Layout tab, in the Rows & Columns group, click **Insert Left**	To create a column to the left of the selected cell. By default, it's the same size as the existing column and has the same formatting. You'll reduce the width of the new column.
Deselect the column	
5 Point to the left edge of the left column, as shown	
Drag to the right until the left column is about 2 picas wide	Drag to about the 96-pica mark on the horizontal ruler. The table will appear to be mostly off the page at this point, but you'll move it back.
6 Point to the left edge of the table until the pointer changes to a four-sided arrow	You'll move the entire table.
Move the table so that it snaps to the left margin guide	Drag the table border to move the table left, until the left edge of the table is aligned with the left margin guide.
7 Drag the right edge of the right column to the left until it lines up with the right margin guide	To fit the table between the page margins.
8 Update the publication	

Merging cells

When you present your data in a table, you might want some cells to span more than one column or row. You do this by merging cells: combining two or more adjacent cells to form a single cell. For example, you might have empty cells that you want to merge into one cell; doing so makes a table less "busy" and helps direct your audience's attention to important information.

To merge cells in a table, select the cells you want to merge. Then, on the Table Tools | Layout tab, click Merge Cells in the Merge group. You can also right-click the selected cells and choose Merge Cells from the shortcut menu.

Splitting cells

When you merge cells, Publisher remembers the original cell configuration. To undo the merge and return the cells to their original layout, place the insertion point in a merged cell and, in the Merge group, click Split Cells. Additionally, you can click Diagonals and choose an option to split a cell diagonally.

B-2: Merging table cells

Here's how	Here's why
1 Drag to select the two cells in the top row of the Spice Tips table	Spice tips / Store spices in a cool, dark
2 On the Layout tab, in the Merge group, click **Merge Cells**	To merge the two cells into one.
Deselect the cell	
3 Update and close the publication	

Topic C: Table formatting

Explanation

After you've created a table, you can apply borders and fills to highlight cells, rows, and columns. You can format table borders of different widths and styles, and you can apply borders to different areas of a table. In addition, you can quickly format an entire table by selecting an option from the Table Formats gallery. You also can position text within cells and insert images into cells.

The Table Formats gallery

You might want to highlight specific columns or rows, or you might want to shade alternate columns or rows to make reading the data easier. You can do this manually, but you might also be able to use one of Publisher's table formats, shown in **Error! Reference source not found.**.

To apply a format to a table, first place the insertion point in the table. Then, on the Table Tools | Design tab, select a style from the Table Formats gallery.

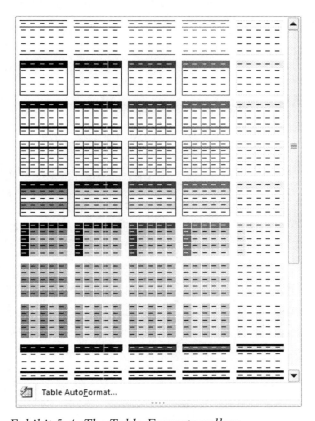

Exhibit 5-4: The Table Formats gallery

Do it!

C-1: Applying table formats

The files for this activity are in Student Data folder **Unit 5\Topic C**.

Here's how	Here's why
1 Open Newsletter 7	
Save the publication as **My newsletter 7**	
2 Go to page 5	
3 Place the insertion point in the table	Click in any cell of the Spice tips table.
4 Click the **Design** tab	
5 In the Table Formats group, click as shown	(The More button.) To display the gallery.
Point to several different table formats	(Do not click the mouse button). As you point to each format, Publisher displays the resulting table format in the document window.
Click the indicated format	Table Style 28.
6 Update the publication	

Cell shading

Explanation   You can apply shading to sections of a table to visually differentiate them from other sections. To do so, first, select the cells you want to shade. Then, on the Table Tools | Design tab, in the Table Formats group, select a color in the Fill gallery.

Do it!   ### C-2:   Shading table cells

Here's how	Here's why
1 Place the insertion point in the indicated cell	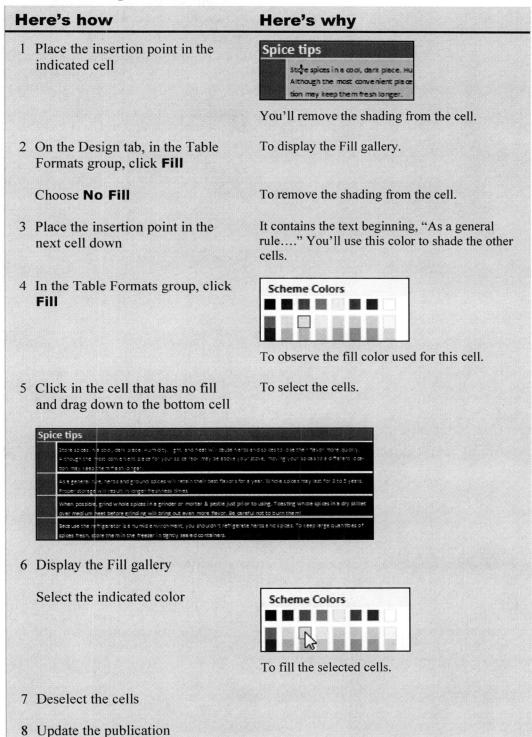 You'll remove the shading from the cell.
2 On the Design tab, in the Table Formats group, click **Fill**	To display the Fill gallery.
Choose **No Fill**	To remove the shading from the cell.
3 Place the insertion point in the next cell down	It contains the text beginning, "As a general rule…." You'll use this color to shade the other cells.
4 In the Table Formats group, click **Fill**	To observe the fill color used for this cell.
5 Click in the cell that has no fill and drag down to the bottom cell	To select the cells.
6 Display the Fill gallery	
Select the indicated color	To fill the selected cells.
7 Deselect the cells	
8 Update the publication	

Aligning text in a table

Explanation

You can align text in table cells by setting vertical and horizontal alignment options or by specifying text box margins so that the text is inset from the table boundaries.

To align text in cells:

1   Select the cell(s) containing text you want to position.

2   Click the Table Tools | Layout tab.

3   To position the text vertically or horizontally in the text box, select an option in the Alignment group, as shown in Exhibit 5-5.

4   To inset the text, click Cell Margins and select an option from the gallery or choose Custom Margins to open the Format Table dialog box.

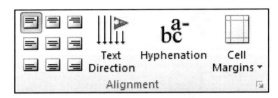

Exhibit 5-5: Cell alignment options

Do it!

C-3: Aligning text within table cells

Here's how	Here's why
1 Place the insertion point in the top cell	You'll inset the text so that it's no longer flush with the left side of the table.
2 On the Layout tab, in the Alignment group, click **Cell Margins** and choose **Custom Margins...**	To open the Format Table dialog box.
3 Under Text Box Margins, edit the Left box to read **1**	To inset the text 1 pica from the left of the cell.
Click **OK**	To close the dialog box. Next, you'll center the text vertically in the remaining rows and inset the text from the right side of the table.
4 Point to the left of the second row, as shown	The pointer changes to a right-pointing arrow, indicating that you can click to select the row, or drag to select multiple rows.
Drag down to select the bottom four rows	
5 In the Alignment group, click **Cell Margins** and choose **Custom Margins...**	
Set the Left and Right margins to **1**, and click **OK**	
6 Update the publication	

Cell border attributes

Explanation

You can increase the color and weight (thickness) of cell borders. You can also hide cell borders so the table does not have a grid-like appearance.

To modify cell borders:

1   Select the cells with borders you want to format.

2   Right-click and choose Format Table to open the Format Table dialog box.

3   Click the Colors and Lines tab, shown in Exhibit 5-6.

4   Under Preview, the border icons show which cell borders the formatting will be applied to. Click the icons to select the borders you want to activate.

5   By default, Publisher creates tables without a visible border. To show the border, select a color from the Color list under the Line heading.

6   If necessary, edit the Weight box to set the thickness of the cell borders.

7   If necessary, repeat steps 3 through 5 for other cell borders. For, example, if you've applied formatting only to the top border, you could deselect it and select another border to apply formatting to, and so on.

8   Click OK.

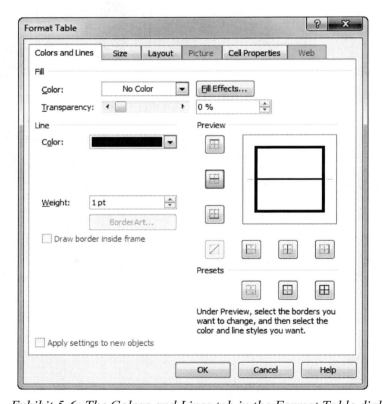

Exhibit 5-6: The Colors and Lines tab in the Format Table dialog box

Do it!

C-4: Formatting cell borders

Here's how	Here's why
1 Select the entire table	The style you selected creates a white border between cells. You'll modify this.
Right-click the table and choose **Format Table...**	To open the Format Table dialog box.
Click the **Colors and Lines** tab	
2 Under Preview, click [ ]	To specify the horizontal border between cells. (The top, bottom, right, and left borders are selected by default.) You'll set the outside borders and the horizontal borders to use a dark red color.
Under Line, from the Color list, select the indicated color	
Edit the Weight box to read **3 pt**	Next, you'll specify settings only for the horizontal border between cells.
3 Click [ ]	To deselect the top border.
4 Deselect the bottom, left, and right borders	(Click the appropriate buttons.) So that only the horizontal border icon is selected.
Set the line weight to **1 pt**	
Click **OK**	
5 Deselect the table	To observe the cell border formatting you've applied.
6 Update the publication	

Graphics in table cells

Explanation

You can place graphics in table cells just as you would elsewhere in a publication. To insert an image in a table cell:

1 On the Insert tab, in the Illustrations group, click Picture. The Insert Picture dialog box opens.

2 Select the picture that you want to insert.

3 Click Insert to insert the graphic.

4 Move the graphic to the desired location in the cell.

Inline images

If you want to position an image inline with text, you have to tell Publisher to treat the graphic as a text character; otherwise, the image will overlap the text. To do so, you need to set the graphic's position to *inline*, as follows:

1 Insert a picture.

2 Drag the picture where you want it in the text.

3 Right-click the picture and choose Format Picture to open the Format Picture dialog box.

4 Click the Layout tab.

5 From the Object Position list, select Inline. (The list will be unavailable if the graphic isn't overlapping a table or text box.)

6 Click OK.

Store spices in a cool, dark place. Humidity, light, and heat will cause herbs and spices to lose their flavor more quickly. Although the most convenient place for your spice rack may be above your stove, moving your spices to a different location may keep them fresh longer.

Exhibit 5-7: An example of a graphic

Do it!

C-5: Inserting graphics into table cells

The files for this activity are in Student Data folder **Unit 5\Topic C**.

Here's how	Here's why
1 On the Insert tab, in the Illustrations group, click **Picture**	To open the Insert Picture dialog box.
Select **Small pepper**	In the current topic folder.
Click **Insert**	To insert the image into the publication.
2 Move the image so that it overlaps the table	You'll set the image's position to inline. To do so, the image has to be overlapping a text box.
3 Right-click the image and choose **Format Picture...**	To open the Format Picture dialog box.
Click the **Size** tab	
Under Scale, edit the Height box to read **75** and press (TAB)	To reduce the image's size to 75% of its actual size.
Click **OK**	
4 Drag the graphic into the left cell of the second row	
5 Increase the size of the left column slightly, as shown	(If necessary.) Notice that increasing the width of the left column increases the overall size of the table, and it now extends beyond the right margin guide.
6 Realign the right edge of the table with the right margin guide	
7 Select the pepper graphic	
Press (CTRL) + (C)	To copy the graphic.
Press (CTRL) + (V)	To create a copy of the graphic.
8 Drag the graphic into the left cell of the third row	

9 Create copies of the pepper graphic for the last two rows	Press Ctrl+V twice more and position the graphics.
Align the graphics as shown	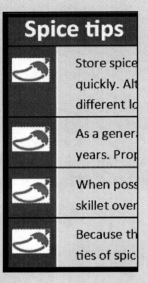
10 Update the publication	

Editing an Excel spreadsheet in Publisher

Explanation   If you've imported an Excel file into a publication, you can use Excel's tools to modify the spreadsheet. By default, Publisher inserts the contents of the Excel file as a table object. When you double-click the table object, you can modify the original and edit its contents using settings, tools, and commands from Excel, as shown in Exhibit 5-8.

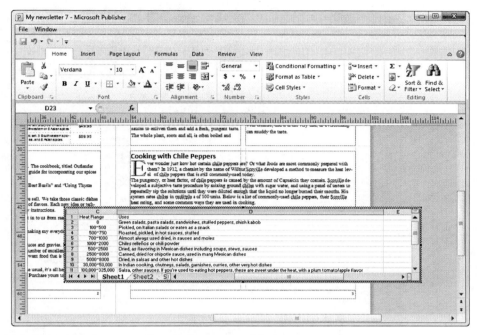

Exhibit 5-8: Editing an Excel object in Publisher

Do it!   ## C-6:   Modifying an Excel spreadsheet

Here's how	Here's why
1 Go to page 3	
Zoom in on the spreadsheet at the bottom of the page	
Double-click the spreadsheet	The Excel application opens within Publisher. You'll delete the blank first column of the sheet.
2 At the bottom of the Excel object, scroll to the left	To view column A.
Right-click the column A heading	To access the shortcut menu.
Choose **Delete**	To delete the column.

3	Click as shown	

		A	B
⊕			
1		Pepper	Heat Range
2		Sweet Bell	0

To select the entire sheet.

	In the Font group, from the Font Size list, select **9**	
4	Click **1**	(In the spreadsheet.) To select the first row.
	Press (CTRL) + (B)	To make the text bold.
5	Right-click the column C heading	
	From the shortcut menu, choose **Column Width...**	To open the Column Width dialog box.
	Edit the Column Width box to read **55**	To set the column width to 55 characters.
	Click **OK**	
6	Right-click the column C heading	
	From the shortcut menu, choose **Format Cells...**	To open the Format Cells dialog box.
7	Click the **Alignment** tab	
	Under Text control, check **Wrap text**	
	Click **OK**	To make the text wrap within the width of the column.
8	Click the document away from the spreadsheet	To return to the document.
9	Move the table to align with the left and bottom page margins	
10	Update and close the publication	

Unit summary: Tables

Topic A   In this topic, you learned how to **create tables**, **navigate** between cells, enter content into table cells, and **import data** from an Excel file.

Topic B   In this topic, you learned how to **insert rows** and **columns**, change the dimensions of rows and columns, and **merge** and **split** cells.

Topic C   In this topic, you learned how to apply **table formatting**, modify **color fills**, **position text** in a table, apply **cell border formatting**, **insert graphics** into table cells, and **edit an Excel spreadsheet** directly in Publisher.

Independent practice activity

In this activity, you'll create and format a new table.

1 Create a new, blank publication and save it as **My tables** in the Unit summary folder.

2 Insert a table with four columns and four rows.

3 Add the text in the first four rows, as shown in Exhibit 5-9. (You'll add the fifth row next.)

4 Add a fifth row to the table.

5 Add the text in the fifth row, as shown in Exhibit 5-9.

6 Apply the table format Table Style 22 to the table. (*Hint*: Use the Table Tools | Design tab.)

7 Change the shade of the first row to a red color.

8 Give the table a **2 pt** outside border.

9 Update and close the publication.

Tea	Vendor	Order status	Comments
Oolong	East Seas	En route	2 weeks late
Darjeeling	China Clipper	In warehouse	Top seller
Earl Grey	House of Lords	In warehouse	Not fresh
House Blend	China Clipper	Ships today	New product

Exhibit 5-9: The table after step 3

Tea	Vendor	Order status	Comments
Oolong	East Seas	En route	2 weeks late
Darjeeling	China Clipper	In warehouse	Top seller
Earl Grey	House of Lords	In warehouse	Not fresh
House Blend	China Clipper	Ships today	New product

Exhibit 5-10: The table after step 8

Review questions

1 In Publisher, you can convert existing text to a table. True or false?

2 To edit an Excel spreadsheet that you inserted into a publication, you first need to:

A Place the insertion point in the table.

B Double-click it.

C Click the Design tab.

D You can't—you have to recreate the table from scratch.

3 When the insertion point is in the rightmost cell in the last row of a table and you press Tab, what happens?

A The insertion point moves to the next available text box.

B Publisher creates a new table.

C Publisher creates a new row.

D Nothing.

4 When merging cells, what happens to the contents of each cell?

5 If you want to insert an image around text without having the image overlap the text, what do you need to do?

A Scale it down.

B Convert it to the TIFF format.

C Convert it to a table image.

D Set its position to inline.

Unit 6

Layout and design techniques

Unit time: 45 minutes

Complete this unit, and you'll know how to:

A Position text in text boxes, apply text box styles and effects, and add columns to text boxes.

B Adjust text wrap for a picture and modify pictures.

C Adjust stacking order and group items.

Topic A: Text boxes

Explanation

As you design documents and publications, you'll often want to adjust the arrangement and alignment of content in your text boxes. For example, you can align text in relation to its text box, and you can apply margins to the inside edges of a text box to add space between the text and the edges of the text box, which improves readability. In addition, you can apply automatic adjustments to get the best fit.

Text box margins and alignment

To position text within a text box:

1   Place the insertion point in the text box.
2   Click the Text Box Tools | Format tab.
3   To position the text vertically or horizontally in the text box, select an option in the Alignment group, as shown in Exhibit 6-1.
4   To inset the text, click Margins and select an option from the gallery or choose Custom Margins to open the Format Text Box dialog box.

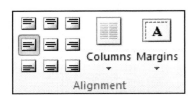

Exhibit 6-1: Text box alignment options

Do it!

A-1: Positioning text within a text box

The files for this activity are in Student Data folder **Unit 6\Topic A**.

Here's how	Here's why
1 Open Newsletter 8	
Save the publication as **My newsletter 8**	In the current topic folder.
2 On page 1, place the insertion point in the text box in the left column	(The text box that contains the list of articles.) You'll adjust the positioning of this text relative to the text box.
Right-click and choose **Zoom, Selected Objects**	To zoom in on the text box.
3 Click the **Text Box Tools | Format** tab	
4 In the Alignment group, click ▤	(The Align Center Left button.) To center the text vertically in the text box.
5 Click **Margins** and select **Wide**	To increase the space between the text box and the text within it. This adjustment causes the tab stops to misalign.
6 Press ⌨CTRL + ⌨A	To select all of the text in the text box.
On the Home tab, click the Paragraph dialog box launcher	
Click the **Tabs** tab	
Edit the Tab stop position box to read **11** and click **Set**; then click **OK**	To set a new tab stop at 11pi.
7 Deselect the text	
Update the publication	

The Text Fit command

Explanation

You might have a layout in which the size of the text box is fixed and you need the text to fit within it. Or you might have a fixed amount of text and need to fit a text box to it. You can use the Text Fit command, on the Text Box Tools | Format tab, to apply automatic adjustments to fit text in a text box.

To do so:

1 Place the insertion point in a text box.

2 Click the Text Box Tools | Format tab.

3 In the Text group, click Text Fit and select an option:

- **Best Fit** – Grows or shrinks the type size of the text to fit within the boundaries of the text box, without modifying the text box itself.

- **Shrink Text On Overflow** – If text overflows a text box, reduces the type size of the text so that it fits in the text box.

- **Grow Text Box to Fit** – If text overflows a text box, increases the size of the text box to fit the text without modifying the type size.

- **Do Not Autofit** – The default setting, which doesn't automatically adjust the text box or the type size.

Once you've applied a Text Fit command, Publisher updates the text or the text box when you make changes. For example, if you apply the Best Fit command and then reduce the size of the text box, Publisher automatically reduces the type size to fit within the new dimensions.

Do it!

A-2: Fitting text to a text box

Here's how	Here's why
1 Place the insertion point in the text box in the left column	If necessary.
2 In the Text group of the Text Box Tools | Format tab, click **Text Fit** and choose **Best Fit**	Publisher increases the type size to fill the text box.
3 Place the insertion point as shown	

You'll insert a reference to another article.

Press ⏎ ENTER	Publisher reduces the type size so that the text still fits in the text box.
Type **From the President**	
Press TAB and type **5**	
Press ⏎ ENTER , type **What's new at Outlander Spices.**, and press ⏎ ENTER	

Publisher reduces the type size again.

4 Update the publication

Text box styles and effects

Explanation

You can apply a number of formatting effects to shapes in Publisher, including text boxes. When a text box is selected, click the Drawing Tools | Format tab to see options for formatting shape styles, shadow effects, and 3-D effects, as shown in Exhibit 6-2.

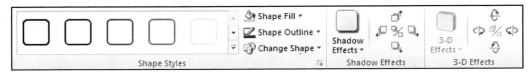

Exhibit 6-2: Shape formatting options on the Drawing Tools | Format tab

By applying a style from the Shape Style gallery, you can quickly format a text box's fill and outline. However, you might want to modify these settings, apply only an outline or fill, or use a format not available in the Shape Style gallery. To do this, choose options from the Shape Fill and Shape Outline menus.

For example, from the Shape Fill menu, you can choose Gradient, More Gradients to open the Fill Effects dialog box. You can create a custom gradient using the colors of your choice. In the Fill Effects dialog box, you can also specify settings for texture, pattern, picture, or tint fills.

Text box outlines

When you apply a style, an outline is usually specified, and you can modify it by selecting an option from the Shape Outline menu. But you can specify more options for an outline by using the Format Text Box dialog box. To do so:

1 Right-click the text box and choose Format Text Box.
2 Click the Colors and Lines tab.
3 Under Preview, the border icons show which cell borders the formatting will be applied to. Click the icons to select the borders you want to activate.
4 Under Line, select a color from the Color list.
5 If desired, select a dashed style from the Dashed list.
6 If desired, select a style from the Style list. Selecting Border Art will open the Border Art dialog box.
7 If desired, edit the Weight box to set the thickness of the cell borders.
8 To draw the border inside the frame, check Draw border inside frame.
9 If necessary, repeat steps 3 through 8 for other border areas. For example, if you've applied formatting only to the top border, then you can deselect it and then select another border to format, and so on.
10 Click OK.

Do it!

A-3: Applying styles to a text box

Here's how	Here's why
1 Click the **Drawing Tools | Format** tab	
2 In the Shape Styles group, click the More button	To display the Shape Styles gallery.
Select the indicated style	Horizontal Gradient – Accent 4.
3 From the Shape Fill menu, choose **Gradient, More Gradients…**	To open the Fill Effects dialog box, with the Gradient tab active.
4 From the Color 1 list, select the indicated color	Light Green.
From the Color 2 list, select the indicated color	Green.
Under Variants, select the indicated style	
Click **OK**	
5 From the Shape Outline gallery, select the indicated color	
6 From the Shadow Effects gallery, select the indicated option	
7 Update the publication	

Multiple-column text boxes

Explanation

If you want to create multiple columns of text, it's typically easier to format a text box with multiple columns than to create multiple text boxes, position them on the layout, and then link each one. To create a text box with multiple columns, select the text box, and then, on the Text Box Tools | Format tab, in the Alignment group, click Columns and select an option.

To format a text box with more than three columns, or to control the amount of spacing between columns:

1   Select the text box.
2   Click the Text Box Tools | Format tab.
3   In the Alignment group, click Columns and choose More Columns to open the Columns dialog box, shown in Exhibit 6-3.
4   Edit the Number box.
5   Edit the Spacing box to adjust the amount of space between columns.
6   Click OK.

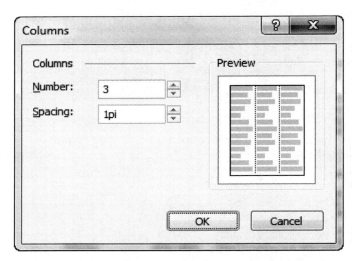

Exhibit 6-3: The Columns dialog box

Do it!   **A-4: Changing text box columns**

Here's how	Here's why
1 Go to page 2	You'll adjust the Cooking with Outlander article at the bottom of the page to flow in three columns.
2 View the whole spread in the window	
3 Select the text box under the heading "Cooking with Outlander"	At the bottom of page 2.
4 Click the **Text Box Tools | Format** tab	
In the Alignment group, click **Columns** and select **Three Columns**	To convert the text box to three columns. The text flows automatically through the three columns.
5 Click **Columns** and select **More Columns...**	To open the Columns dialog box.
Edit the Spacing box to read **1**	To specify 1 pica of space between columns.
Click **OK**	
6 Update and close the publication	

Topic B: Graphics adjustments

Explanation

After you've inserted graphics, you can move them, change the way text wraps around them, and resize, rotate, and crop them. You can also change a graphic's contrast, brightness, and compression.

If you want to rotate, resize, or crop a graphic, it's often best to perform these types of transformations in the graphics application originally used to create the graphic. If that's not possible, however, you can make some changes directly in Publisher.

Text wrapping

Text wrapping forces any text behind an object to flow around it so that the text is not hidden. By default, Publisher doesn't apply wrapping to text boxes, but it does apply wrapping to picture frames by default. A picture frame that overlaps text will automatically force text to wrap around it.

You can change how text wraps, or flows, around a graphic. Using the Wrap Text menu in the Arrange group, you can select the options shown in Exhibit 6-4.

Exhibit 6-4: The Wrap Text menu

You can control a graphic's positioning and text wrapping with greater precision by using the Format Picture dialog box. For example, you can specify the text-wrap distance.

To specify text-wrap distance values for a selected graphic:

1   On the Picture Tools | Format tab, in the Arrange group, click Wrap Text and choose More Layout Options to open the Format Picture dialog box with the Layout tab active, as shown in Exhibit 6-5.

2   If necessary, under Wrapping Style, select Square. ("Distance from text" options will only be available if this is selected.)

3   Under "Distance from text," clear Automatic and specify the minimum distance between text and each side of the graphic.

4   Click OK.

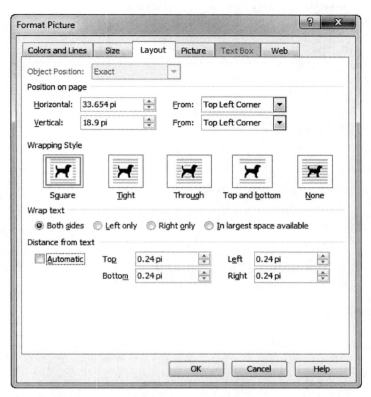

Exhibit 6-5: The Format Picture dialog box, showing text wrapping options

Do it!

B-1: Controlling text wrap

The files for this activity are in Student Data folder **Unit 6\Topic B**.

Here's how	Here's why
1 Open Newsletter 9	
Save the publication as **My newsletter 9**	
2 Go to page 2	
3 On the Insert tab, click **Picture**	
Select **Cookbook** and click **Insert**	
4 Position the picture between the first two columns, as shown	
5 In the Arrange group, click **Wrap Text** and choose **More Layout Options...**	To open the Format Picture dialog box.
6 Under Wrapping Style, verify that Square is selected	
7 Under Distance from text, clear **Automatic**	
Edit the Top, Left, Bottom, and Right boxes to read **1**	To add 1 pica of space between the picture frame and the text wrapping around it.
Click **OK**	The picture frame now has 1 pica of space on all four sides, creating space between it and the text, which improves its appearance and the article's readability.
8 Hold (CTRL) and drag a corner resize handle on the picture	To reduce its size from the center point.
Resize the picture to 8 pi wide	So that the text doesn't overflow the text box.
9 Update the publication	

Picture adjustments

In addition to changing the location and size of a graphic, you can change its color, contrast, and brightness. To do so, use the options in the Adjust group (on the Picture Tools | Format tab), shown in Exhibit 6-6.

Exhibit 6-6: The Adjust group on the Picture Tools | Format tab

To change a selected graphic's contrast and brightness, use the Brightness and Contrast galleries. At any time, you can return the graphic to its original settings by clicking Reset Picture.

Picture compression

You can apply compression to a picture to adjust its file size and quality. In the Adjust group, click Compress Pictures to open the Compress Pictures dialog box. Here, you can specify whether to apply settings to the selected graphic or to all graphics in the publication.

In the Compress Pictures dialog box, you can choose to delete cropped areas of a picture. You can also select the optimum quality of the image—the number of pixels per inch (ppi)—based on its purpose. For example, you can select the Commercial Printing option if you intend to print the document containing the image. This compression level is sufficient for paper output. However, if you want to send the document through e-mail, you'll want a smaller file size and can select the Web option.

Picture styles

You can apply styles to pictures to create borders, reflections, and other effects. To do so, select a picture; then, in the Picture Styles group on the Picture Tools | Format tab, select the desired style from the gallery.

Do it!

B-2: Adjusting brightness and applying picture styles

Here's how	Here's why
1 On page 2, select the cookbook image	If necessary.
2 In the Adjust group, click **Brightness** and select **-10%**	To reduce the picture's brightness.
3 In the Picture Styles group, display the gallery	
Select the indicated style	Picture Style 23.
4 In the Picture Styles group, click **Picture Border** and select the indicated color	
5 Click **Caption** and select the indicated option	(Tint – Layout 1.) To add a caption to the picture.
6 Right-click the picture and choose **Zoom**, **Selected Objects**	
7 Below the picture, click **Picture caption**	To select the placeholder text.
Type **Our new cookbook**	
8 Update the publication	

The Recolor command

Explanation

You can change the color of a picture by clicking Recolor in the Adjust group and selecting an option from the gallery. In the Recolor gallery, you can also choose More Variations to open the Recolor Picture dialog box. In addition, you can choose Set Transparent Color and then click part of the image to make it transparent.

Do it!

B-3:   Recoloring a picture

Here's how	Here's why
1 Go to page 5	
Right-click the table and choose **Zoom, Selected Objects**	The pepper images contain white backgrounds. They would look better if the background matched the red fill in the table.
2 Select the first pepper picture	
3 In the Adjust group, click **Recolor** and choose **Set Transparent Color**	(On the Picture Tools | Format tab.) The cursor changes to indicate that you can click to select a color to make transparent.
Click the indicated area	To make the white background in the picture transparent.
4 Click **Recolor** and point to the options in the gallery	To see the effects of recoloring the picture.
Select the indicated option	**Dark Variations**
5 Select the next pepper	
6 Make the white area transparent	In the Adjust group, click Recolor and choose Set Transparent Color. Then click the white area in the picture.
7 Recolor the picture	To make it the same as the other picture you recolored.
8 Make the white areas in the other pepper pictures transparent	
9 Recolor the remaining peppers	To give them a red color.
10 Update and close the publication	

Topic C: Stacking and grouping objects

Explanation

As you add pictures and text to your layout, some boxes might overlap each other. For example, you might want to move an object behind a picture frame but not behind a graphic that you're using for a background image. To solve layout issues like this, you can group objects and control their stacking order.

Grouping and ungrouping objects

Explanation

You can group multiple objects so that they can be manipulated as a single unit. To group objects, select all the objects you want in the group by pressing Shift and clicking on each object. Then, on the Home tab, in the Arrange box, click Group. The objects will then act as one item—when you select one of the grouped objects, all the objects in the group are selected. To ungroup objects, select the group and click Ungroup, in the Arrange group.

When you select grouped objects, a selection boundary appears around all of the objects, as shown in Exhibit 6-7.

Exhibit 6-7: Ungrouped (left) and grouped (right) objects

Do it!

C-1: Grouping objects

The files for this activity are in Student Data folder **Unit 6\Topic C**.

Here's how	Here's why
1 Open Newsletter 10	
Save the publication as **My newsletter 10**	
2 Go to page 4	
3 At the bottom of the page, select the picture of Stephanie Green	
Press and hold (SHIFT)	
Click the text box under the picture	To select this item along with the picture.
4 Click the **Home** tab	
In the Arrange group, click **Group**	Now that the objects are grouped, they can be moved or resized as a single unit.
5 Move the group over the blue rectangle, as shown	
	While you're dragging the group, it's visible. However, once you release the mouse button, the grouped objects disappear behind the rectangle. You'll adjust the stacking order to correct this.
6 Update the publication	

Within the image:

"I hope you enjoy this month's recipe. It's our family's favorite!"

—Stephanie Green

Controlling object overlapping

Each new object you create is positioned at the top of the "stacking order" by default. This means new objects overlap existing objects. However, you might want an object that's in front of another object to appear behind it instead.

To change the stacking order of objects:

1 Select the object that you want to move forward or backward in the stacking order.

2 Click the Home tab.

2 In the Arrange group, select an option:

- Click Bring Forward to move the selected object forward one position in the stacking order.

- Click Send Backward to move the selected object back one position in the stacking order.

- Display the Bring Forward menu and choose Bring to Front to move the selected object in front of every other object on the page.

- Display the Send Backward menu and choose Send to Back to move the selected object behind every other object on the page.

Do it!

C-2: Stacking objects

Here's how	Here's why
1 Click the blue rectangle	To select it (and to deselect the grouped objects, if they're still selected).
2 In the Arrange group, display the Send Backward menu and choose **Send to Back**	The rectangle is now behind the plate image, but it needs to be in front of it.
3 In the Arrange group, click **Bring Forward**	To move the selected object forward one level in the stacking order. This puts it in front of the plate image.
4 Update and close the publication	

Unit summary: Layout and design techniques

Topic A   In this topic, you learned how to control the **alignment** of text in a text box, apply **text box margins,** and apply **styles and effects** to text boxes. Then, you learned how to create **multiple-column text boxes.**

Topic B   In this topic, you learned how to control **text wrapping** around a picture and to adjust pictures' **brightness, contrast, color,** and **compression.**

Topic C   In this topic, you learned how to **group** and **ungroup** objects and how to control the **stacking order** of objects. You learned that grouping multiple objects enables you to manipulate them all as a single unit.

Independent practice activity

In this activity, you'll set text box margins, and you'll apply a fill color and a border to a text box. Then you'll convert a text box to a multiple-column format, and, finally, you'll adjust the text wrap for a picture.

The files for this activity are in Student Data folder **Unit 6\Unit summary.**

1 Open **Note 4,** and save it as **My note 4.**

2 Go to page 5 and add a light green fill color to the recipe text box.

3 Apply a **2 pi** margin on all four sides of the text box.

4 Give the text box a **solid, 4pt, dark green** border. Compare your text box to the one shown in Exhibit 6-8.

5 Go to page 4. Convert the text box to a two-column text box, with **1 pi** of spacing between the columns.

6 Go to page 2. Move the picture of the president to the front, so that the text flows around it.

7 Adjust the text wrap for the picture so that the text flows **1 pi** from the picture frame.

8 Update and close the publication.

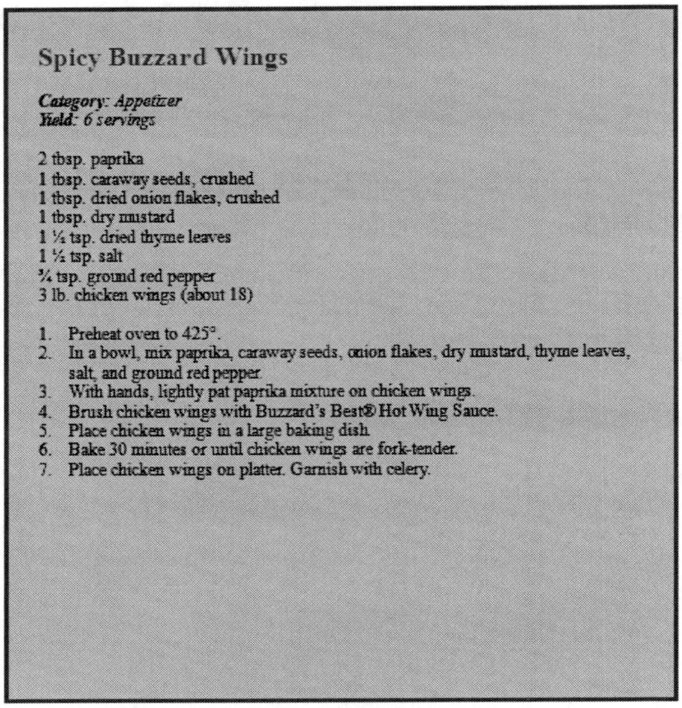

Spicy Buzzard Wings

Category: Appetizer
Yield: 6 servings

2 tbsp. paprika
1 tbsp. caraway seeds, crushed
1 tbsp. dried onion flakes, crushed
1 tbsp. dry mustard
1 ¼ tsp. dried thyme leaves
1 ¼ tsp. salt
¾ tsp. ground red pepper
3 lb. chicken wings (about 18)

1. Preheat oven to 425°.
2. In a bowl, mix paprika, caraway seeds, onion flakes, dry mustard, thyme leaves, salt, and ground red pepper.
3. With hands, lightly pat paprika mixture on chicken wings.
4. Brush chicken wings with Buzzard's Best® Hot Wing Sauce.
5. Place chicken wings in a large baking dish.
6. Bake 30 minutes or until chicken wings are fork-tender.
7. Place chicken wings on platter. Garnish with celery.

Exhibit 6-8: The recipe text box on page 5 after step 4

Review questions

1 You have a text box that needs to be a specific size to fit in a layout, but the text in it doesn't quite fill the text box. Which Text Fit command could you use to solve this problem?

   A Best Fit

   B Shrink Text on Overflow

   C Grow Text Box to Fit

   D Do Not Autofit

2 Publisher provides shape styles that you can use to apply preset fill and stroke combinations to text boxes. How can you modify these styles after you apply them?

   A Select an option from the Shape Fill menu.

   B Select an option from the Shape Outline menu.

   C Right-click the text box and choose Format Text Box.

   D All of the above.

3 You wan to adjust the distance between a picture and the text that wraps around it. How can you do this?

   A Drag the picture's adjustment handles to resize it.

   B On the Picture Tools | Format tab, in the Arrange group, click Wrap Text and choose Top and Bottom.

   C In the Format Picture dialog box, clear Automatic and specify values in the Top, Bottom, Left, and Right boxes.

   D You can't. Publisher always sets the text wrap automatically.

4 Which of the following can you NOT adjust using Publisher's Adjust commands on the Picture Tools | Format tab?

   A Brightness

   B Color

   C Sharpness

   D Compression

5 Which one of the following commands will place a selected object on top of every other object in the stacking order?

   A Bring Forward

   B Bring to Front

   C Place on Top

   D Move Up

6 Explain what happens when you select one item that has been grouped with others.

Unit 7

Finalizing publications

Unit time: 45 minutes

Complete this unit, and you'll know how to:

A Print publications and export publications to PDF format.

B Check spelling, apply design checks, and prepare a publication for commercial printing.

Topic A: Publication output

Explanation

Publisher's primary purpose is to create documents for print, which can range from a four-color print run at a professional print shop to several copies on your own laser or inkjet printer. You might also want to generate a copy of a layout as a PDF file so that you can preview and share the publication before it's printed.

Print options

Before you print a publication, you can preview it and specify settings. To preview a document before printing, click the File tab and then click Print, or press Ctrl+P. Specify the number of copies, the printer, which pages to print, and other settings. The preview window shows you what the document will look like when it's printed. When you're ready to send the publication to the printer, click Print.

The Print settings on the File tab, shown in Exhibit 7-1, provide a number of options you can set when printing a publication. You can change the printer, print specific pages, print multiple copies, and print multiple pages on a single sheet of paper. (Different options might be available, depending on the printer you select.)

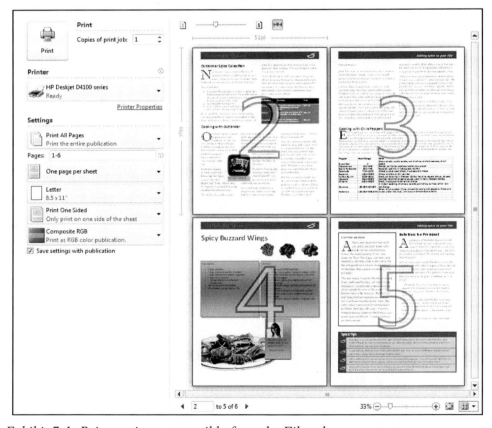

Exhibit 7-1: Print settings, accessible from the File tab

Do it!

A-1:   Printing a publication

The files for this activity are in Student Data folder **Unit 7\Topic A**.

Here's how	Here's why
1 Open Newsletter 11	
Save the publication as **My newsletter 11**	In the current topic folder.
2 Click the **File** tab	
Click **Print**	(Or press Ctrl+P.) To display print options and a preview of the document.
3 Observe the options under Settings	You can specify which pages will print, and you can choose other options depending on the layout you select.
4 At the top-left of the preview, drag the slider as shown	To show the page number superimposed in the preview. These page numbers won't print.
5 At the bottom-left of the preview, click ▶	(The Next Sheet button.) To go to the next page.
6 At the bottom-right of the preview, click 🔳 and select **2 x 2**, as shown	(The View Multiple Sheets button.) To view multiple pages of the document.
7 Under Settings, click **Composite RGB** and select **Composite Grayscale**	To print the publication in black and white. If you're previewing the layout, this is a good way to save printer ink.
8 If you are connected to a printer, click **Print**	To print the current document. If your computer is not connected to a printer, press Esc instead.
9 Update the document	

PDF and XPS documents

Explanation

In addition to printing a publication, you might also need to e-mail a copy of it to a coworker or post it online for review. You do so by saving a publication as a static document. A static document is one that can't be edited as easily as a Publisher file. Saving a publication as a static document provides two major advantages:

- Users who receive a static document don't need to have Publisher to read it. Static documents can be read in viewers that can be downloaded free of charge.
- A static document can't be altered easily. The author can be certain that the publication content remains unchanged before passing it on.

You can save a publication in either of two static-document formats:

- **PDF** — Files saved in Adobe's PDF format can be viewed with the Adobe Reader application, as shown in Exhibit 7-2 or with another PDF reader.
- **XPS** — Files saved in Microsoft's XML-based XPS format can be viewed in XPS Viewer.

To save a publication as a static document:

1 On the File tab, click Save & Send.
2 Under File Types, click Create PDF/XPS Document.
3 Click "Create PDF/XPS" to open the Publish as PDF or XPS dialog box.
4 Edit the file name as needed.
5 In the Save as type list, select either PDF or XPS Document.
6 *(Optional)* Select an optimization setting.
7 *(Optional)* Click Options to specify how the publication will be printed or distributed, how to manage picture resolution, and other options. Then click OK.
8 Click Publish.

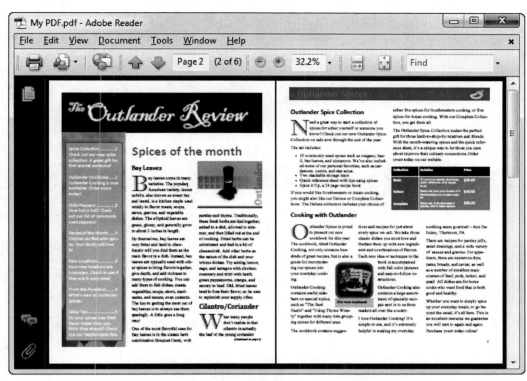

Exhibit 7-2: Adobe Reader, displaying a PDF file created from a publication

Do it!

A-2: Saving a publication as a PDF document

Here's how	Here's why
1 Click the **File** tab	You'll save the publication in a format that can be viewed but not altered by users.
Click **Save & Send**	
2 Under File Types, click **Create PDF/XPS Document**	
Click **Create PDF/XPS**	Create PDF/XPS To open the Publish as PDF or XPS dialog box.
3 Edit the File name box to read **My PDF**	
In the Save as type list, verify that **PDF** is selected	
Verify that **Open file after publishing** is checked	
Click **Publish**	The publication is saved in the PDF file format. Adobe Reader opens and displays the file.
4 Click anywhere in the document	You can place the insertion point in the document and select text or objects, but you cannot edit them.
5 Click	To go to page 2.
6 Choose **View**, **Page Display**, **Two Page View**	To view the spread in the Adobe Reader window.
7 Close Adobe Reader	
8 Update and close the publication	

Topic B: Print preparation

Explanation

Before you distribute a publication, you should proof it carefully, including giving it a thorough spelling check.

Check spelling

By default, Publisher checks your spelling as you type. If you type a word that the program identifies as a possible misspelling, a wavy red line appears under the word. To correct your mistake, you can right-click the word and choose the correct spelling from a list of options in the shortcut menu.

In some cases, the wavy red line might appear under correctly spelled words, such as the name of a person or a place. If you want the spelling checker to ignore such words, you have two options. First, you can right-click the word and choose Ignore All. This command prevents the word from being identified as a possible misspelling in the current publication only. Also, this command applies only to the current session. The next time you open the publication, Publisher will again identify the word as a possible misspelling.

You also can right-click the word and choose Add to Dictionary. This command adds the word to a custom dictionary so that Publisher won't identify it as misspelled again—even in other publications.

The Check Spelling dialog box

You can also check your spelling by using the Check Spelling dialog box, shown in Exhibit 7-3, which provides spelling suggestions that you can accept or ignore. To open this dialog box, click the View tab and, in the Proofing group, click Spelling. Or you can simply press F7. To correct a word flagged as a possible misspelling:

- If the correct word is listed in the Suggestions box, select it and click Change. If the word is misspelled more than once, you can click Change All to change all occurrences of the word.

- Click Ignore or Ignore All to leave the word spelled the way it is.

- Click Add to add the word to the custom dictionary so it will be recognized as correct in future spelling checks.

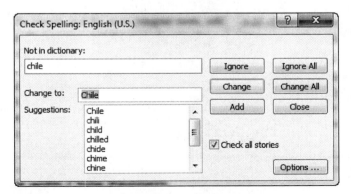

Exhibit 7-3: The Check Spelling dialog box

Do it!

B-1: Checking spelling

The files for this activity are in Student Data folder **Unit 7\Topic B**.

Here's how	Here's why
1 Open Newsletter 12	
Save the publication as **My newsletter 12**	
2 Click the **Review** tab	
In the Proofing group, click **Spelling**	An alert box might appear, indicating that Publisher has finished checking the current story.
Click **Yes**	(If necessary.) To open the Check Spelling dialog box. The first word flagged is "chile." Publisher lists possible correct spellings in the Suggestions list.
3 From the Suggestions list, select **chili**	
Click **Change All**	To change all instances of this word in the publication. The next word flagged is "Scoville." You'll add the word to the custom dictionary, since it likely will appear in this or other publications you produce.
4 Click **Add**	Publisher flags the word "chiles" and, in the Change to box, suggests the correct spelling.
5 Click **Change All**	Publisher flags "comng" and suggests the correct spelling.
6 Click **Change**	Publisher flags the abbreviation "Phila."
7 Edit the Change to box to read **Philadelphia** and click **Change**	The next word flagged is "Salinksy." Because this is a proper name, and won't be used often, you can ignore it.
8 Click **Ignore**	The next flagged word is the Latin "laurus."
9 Click **Ignore**	
10 Continue correcting flagged words, using the appropriate correction option	Ignore "nobilis," "Gami," "coriandrum," and "sativum." Correct "coolking." Ignore "Salinsky." When finished, an alert box appears, indicating that the spelling check is complete.
Click **OK**	
11 Update the document	

The Design Checker

Explanation

With the Design Checker, you can check your publication for problems before you publish it. To access it, click the File tab and, in the Info section, click Run Design Checker to open the Design Checker pane. A list of problems appears, based on the options selected in the Design Checker pane.

Design Checker options

You can select specific items to check for by clicking Design Checker Options at the bottom of the Design Checker pane to open the Design Checker Options dialog box, shown in Exhibit 7-4. The Design Checker is composed of four general categories, as described in the following table.

Option	Description
Run general design checks	Select this option if you want to check for typical design errors, such as objects that are partially off the page, empty text boxes, low-resolution pictures, and overflowing text.
Run commercial printing checks	Select this option if you want to check for problems before you send a publication to a commercial printer.
Run web site checks	Select this option if you intend to publish your document on the Web.
Run e-mail checks	With this option, you can check for email-related issues.

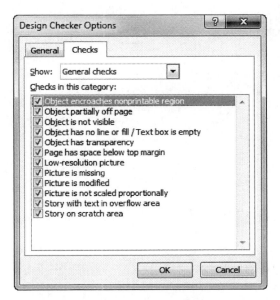

Exhibit 7-4: General Design Checker Options

Fixing problems

When you select options in the Design Checker pane, the list of results is updated automatically. When you fix an item, it's removed from the list. Each item in the list includes a brief description of the problem and its location. To fix an item, right-click the entry and select an option. If the item can't be fixed automatically, select Go to this Item so that you can fix it manually. If you need more information about the nature of the problem, right-click the item and select Explain to open Publisher Help.

Do it!

B-2:   Checking a design for errors

The files for this activity are in Student Data folder **Unit 7\Topic B**.

Here's how	Here's why
1 Click the **File** tab	The Info section is selected by default.
Click **Run Design Checker**	To open the Design Checker pane. Publisher scans the document for design issues.
2 Observe the Design Checker pane	By default, only the first option is selected. You'll check for commercial printing issues as well.
Check **Run commercial printing checks**	Publisher includes issues that might affect the publication when it is sent to a commercial press.
3 Observe the first item in the list	The Design Checker indicates that the publication is in RGB mode, which is not optimal for print publishing. You'll fix this problem to convert the color mode to CMYK.
Click as shown	A shortcut menu appears.
Choose **Fix: Convert to another color mode...**	The Color Model dialog box opens.
4 Select **Process colors (CMYK)**	An alert box appears, indicating that the colors will be converted to process colors.
Click **OK**	
Click **OK**	To close the Color Model dialog box.
	Publisher rechecks the publication and then updates the list of possible issues.

5	Select the new first item in the list	To go to it in the publication. Publisher indicates that this is a low-resolution image.
	On the Picture Tools | Format tab, in the Adjust group, click **Change Picture** and choose **Change Picture...**	To open the Insert Picture dialog box.
	Select **Contents bkgd hi-res** and click **Insert**	To replace the picture. After a few moments, Publisher updates the Design Checker to show that this problem has been resolved.
6	Select the new first item in the list	To go to the image in the publication.
	Click **Change Picture** and choose **Change Picture...**	
	Select **Cinnamon hi-res** and click **Insert**	
7	After Publisher updates the Design Checker list, replace the other two spice images	Select the item in the list. Then click Change Picture and choose Change Picture. Select the "hi-res" version of the appropriate picture and click Insert.
8	Select the remaining design issue	To go to page 6. This page is intentionally blank.
9	Close the Design Checker pane	
10	Update the publication	

The Pack and Go Wizard

Explanation

You can prepare your publication for transfer to another computer or to a commercial printing service by using the Pack and Go Wizard. The Pack and Go Wizard checks your publication for errors that could affect a publication during the printing process after you've sent it to a commercial print vendor. It also collects information about the publication and can automatically produce a PDF version of the document. It collects all relevant information, along with a copy of the original publication, into a compressed ZIP file, which you can then send to your commercial printer.

You should always run the Design Checker before you use the Pack and Go Wizard, to ensure that the publication you send to a printer does not contain critical errors.

To pack a publication for a commercial printer:

1 Click the File tab.

2 Click Save & Send.

3 Under Pack and Go, click Save for a Commercial Printer.

4 Under Save for a Commercial Printer, from the first list, select the appropriate option.

- **Commercial Press** – Creates the highest-quality file, suitable for a commercial printing press, but also creates the largest file size.

- **High quality printing** – Creates a file suitable for sending to a desktop printer or copy shop.

- **Standard** – Creates a file suitable for online use.

- **Minimum size** – Creates a small file suitable for viewing on a monitor.

5 Select an option from the second list to specify which files to package—both PDF and the Publisher file, only PDF, or only a copy of the Publisher file.

6 Click Pack and Go Wizard to open the Pack and Go Wizard dialog box. Follow the steps to complete the Pack and Go process.

Do it!

B-3: Preparing a publication for commercial printing

Here's how	Here's why
1 Click the **File** tab	
Click **Save & Send**	
2 Under Pack and Go, click **Save for a Commercial Printer**	To view the options for sending the file. You'll use the defaults—"Commercial Press" and "Both PDF and Publisher .pub files."
3 Click **Pack and Go Wizard**	To open the Pack and Go Wizard dialog box.
4 Select **Other location**	
Click **Browse...**	
Navigate to the current topic folder and click **OK**	
5 Click **Next**	After a few moments, the wizard indicates that the publication is successfully packed.
6 Clear **Print a composite proof**	
Click **OK**	
7 In Windows Explorer, navigate to the current topic folder	
Verify that a file named My newsletter 12 exists	This is the ZIP file created by the Pack and Go wizard. It contains information for a print service provider, including the original publication and a PDF of the publication.
8 Update and close the publication	In Publisher.

Unit summary: Finalizing publications

Topic A   In this topic, you learned how **preview and print a publication**. You also learned how to export a publication to **PDF**. You learned that the PDF and XPS formats enable you to share your publications with anybody.

Topic B   In this topic, you learned how to make spelling corrections as you work in a publication and how to use the **Check Spelling** dialog box to perform a publication-wide spelling check. You also learned how to use the **Design Checker** to locate and fix problems in your publication. Finally, you learned how to use the **Pack and Go Wizard** to prepare your publication for transfer to another computer or to a commercial printing service.

Independent practice activity

In this activity, you'll open a publication and check for spelling errors. Then you'll create a PDF version of the document and package it for a commercial printer.

The files for this activity are in Student Data folder **Unit 7\Unit summary**.

1 Open Note 5 and save it as **My note 5**.

2 Check for spelling errors in the publication and correct any errors you find.

3 Create a PDF version of the publication, and save it with the same name. When you're done, close Adobe Reader.

4 Using the Design Checker, prepare the publication for a commercial press by changing it from RGB mode to CMYK mode. (*Hint*: Remember to enable the appropriate options in the Design Checker pane.)

5 Using the Design Checker, replace the low-resolution pictures.

6 Using the Design Checker, locate and fix the remaining design issue. (Ignore any "blank space beneath the top margin" design issues if they appear.)

7 Use the Pack and Go Wizard to collect all the information and files for a commercial printing service. Save the file in the current topic folder.

8 Update and close the publication.

9 Close Publisher.

Review questions

1 What are some advantages to exporting a file to PDF or XPS?

2 When using the Check Spelling dialog box, if Publisher thinks a name is a misspelled word, you can click Ignore All, and Publisher will ignore all instances of that name in all publications. True or false?

3 If you encounter a spelling error but you want to instruct Publisher to treat it as an acceptable word in all publications, what command should you use in the Check Spelling dialog box?

   A Change

   B Ignore

   C Ignore All

   D Add

4 If an item found by the Design Checker can't be fixed automatically (by right-clicking it and selecting an option to fix it), what should you do?

5 You should always run the Design Checker before you use the Pack and Go Wizard. True or false?

Course summary

This summary contains information to help you bring the course to a successful conclusion. Using this information, you will be able to:

A Use the summary text to reinforce what you've learned in class.

B Determine the next courses in this series (if any), as well as any other resources that might help you continue to learn about Microsoft Publisher 2010.

Topic A: Course summary

Use the following summary text to reinforce what you've learned in class.

Unit summaries

Unit 1

In this unit, you learned how to **start Publisher** and **open a publication**. You also learned about the **Ribbon,** the **Quick Access toolbar,** and **Backstage view.** Next, you learned how to **navigate** a publication, how to **zoom** in and out, and how to **select text.** Finally, you used **Publisher Help** to search for information on a specific topic.

Unit 2

In this unit, you learned how to **create a new publication,** adjust **margin guides,** set **units of measurement,** insert and format **text,** and adjust text boxes. Then you learned how to insert and modify a **picture.** You also learned how to create and apply **custom colors.** Next, you learned how to use **guides** and the **Measurement task pane.** Finally, you learned how to **align** and **distribute** objects.

Unit 3

In this unit, you created a **facing-pages publication,** set **margin guides,** inserted new pages into a publication, and moved items between publications. You also learned how to work with **master pages** and to set **column guides.** Finally, you set automatic **page numbering** and **applied master pages** to the pages of a publication.

Unit 4

In this unit, you learned how to **link and unlink text boxes** and to create **continuation notices.** You also learned how to create **tab stops** and a **leader,** create and adjust **indents,** apply and format **bullets,** set **keep settings,** control **vertical spacing** and **paragraph spacing,** and create **drop caps.**

Unit 5

In this unit, you learned how to **create tables** and **import data** from an Excel file. Then you learned how to **insert and modify rows** and **columns** and how to **merge** and **split** cells. Next, you learned how to apply **table formatting,** modify **color fills, position text** in a table, apply **cell border formatting, insert graphics** into table cells, and **edit an Excel spreadsheet** directly in Publisher.

Unit 6

In this unit, you learned how to control **alignment,** apply **margins,** apply **styles and effects,** and create **multiple columns** in **text boxes.** You also learned how to control **text wrapping** and to **adjust pictures.** Next, you learned how to **group** and **ungroup** objects and how to control the **stacking order** of objects.

Unit 7

In this unit, you learned how **preview and print a publication** and how to export a publication to **PDF.** You also learned how to use the **Check Spelling** dialog box. Next, you learned how to use the **Design Checker** and the **Pack and Go Wizard.**

Topic B: Continued learning after class

It is impossible to learn how to use any software effectively in a single day. To get the most out of this class, students should begin working with Microsoft Publisher 2010 to perform real tasks as soon as possible. We also offer resources for continued learning.

Next courses in this series

This is the first course in this series. The next course in this series is:

- *Publisher 2010: Advanced*
    - Create advanced publication layouts, edit business information, customize colors, work with the Content Library, and use the Graphics Manager.
    - Use styles, work with WordArt and graphics, align text, and insert special characters.
    - Create sections in a publication and use bookmarks.
    - Use mail merge.
    - Create interactive forms.
    - Add interactive elements for web publication and publish a web site.

Other resources

For more information, visit www.axzopress.com.

Glossary

Backstage view

The view displayed when you click the File tab to display options for working with a publication—such as opening, saving, closing, printing, sharing, and more.

Color separations

Grayscale representations of at least the four process colors cyan, magenta, yellow, and black.

Composite printer

Printers that combine inks directly onto paper to produce a range of colors. Inkjet printers, laser printers, and color copiers fall into this category.

Contextual Ribbon tabs

Ribbon tabs containing specific commands and options that appear only when the objects they control—such as text boxes, pictures, or tables—are selected.

Dialog Box Launcher

The button at the bottom-right of some tab groups that opens a dialog box containing more settings.

Drop cap

Typographic elements, typically an oversized initial letter, that extend down into a paragraph by two or more lines.

Gallery

A type of menu or list that provides icons or other graphics to show the results of commands or options, rather than providing just a list of option names.

Gutter

The place where the bound pages meet—the inside of the spread. Sometimes, the space between columns of text also is referred to as the gutter.

Leader

A series of dots, dashes, lines, or bullets preceding a tab stop.

Live Preview

The Office feature that temporarily displays, in the document, the results of an option as you point to it in a list or gallery.

Margin guides

Visible guidelines around the top, bottom, and sides of each page in a publication. You use margin guides to help position page elements. They do not print, and objects can overlap the margin boundaries and extend to or beyond the edge of the page.

Master page

Acts as a template for pages within a publication. Any items on a master page will automatically be added to pages in a publication to which the master page is applied.

Orphan

The last line in a paragraph displayed as the first line of a column or page, while all of the preceding lines of the paragraph are on the previous column or page.

PDF (Portable Document Format)

A file format that preserves formatting and enables file sharing. PDF provides a standard format for use by commercial printers.

Pica

A unit of measure generally used in publishing, in which 6 picas equals 1 inch, and 1 pica equals 12 points.

Points

A unit of measure used in publishing. For example, font size is measured in points; 72 points equals 1 inch, and 12 points equals 1 pica.

Prepress

The process of preparing a document for printing by separating it into color plates.

Process colors

The inks, represented by the acronym CMYK, used to produce images and color on a composite printer.

Quick Access toolbar

A toolbar displaying buttons for frequently used commands (by default, Save, Undo, and Repeat/Redo). Can be customized.

Ribbon

An interface component that contains the File, Home, Insert, Page Design, Mailings, Review, and View tabs, as well as contextual tabs. Each tab contains several groups of related commands.

Ribbon groups

Collections of related tools and commands displayed on the Ribbon. For example, some tools for formatting text are arranged together in the Font group.

Scratch area

The extra space around the page area that's used for storing text and graphics. Objects in the scratch area won't appear in the printed publication.

Spread

In a facing-pages layout, the pages that a reader would see when the publication is opened.

Text box

Used to place and arrange text on a layout. To work with text, you first have to create a space for that text by creating a text box.

Text wrapping

An attribute that causes text behind an object to flow around it so the text is not covered.

Widow

The first line in a paragraph left as the last line of a column or page, while the remaining lines of the paragraph appear on the following column or page.

XPS (XML Paper Specification)

A file format that preserves formatting and graphics when the file is exported.

Index

100

other stuff

See the big picture, plus
project creativity, resources
and design notes.

"THE NICE THING ABOUT TEAMWORK IS THAT YOU ALWAYS HAVE OTHERS ON YOUR SIDE"
MARGARET CARTY

Simple Scrapbooks

you're the best

4

It sort of blows my mind that I get to work with so many cool people on so many cool projects and call it a job. The editors and designers at *Simple Scrapbooks* are not just my colleagues, they are my team—in fact, I don't believe there is another group of people anywhere more concerned with editorial quality and integrity, or more committed to a vision. I love sharing ideas with these people. With them I feel safe and understood and appreciated. So, lest anyone think I pulled this book thing off by myself, please know that nothing worth doing should ever be done alone.

Respect your fellow human beings, treat them fairly, disagree with them honestly, enjoy their friendship, explore your thoughts about one another candidly, work together for a common goal and help one another achieve it.
BILL BRADLEY

thanks, team.

I couldn't do it without you!

P.S. This book is dedicated to Don and Deanna Lambson for believing in me; but mostly for being an example of overwhelming kindness and generosity.

P.P.S. Truth be told, you are holding this book due in large part to MaryRuth Francks and her willingness to work very odd hours. Thanks, friend!

One more thing—Cathy, you're a genius.

think big!

I've titled this book **The Big Picture** for three reasons. First, I want to help you recognize and begin to record the many aspects of life that can become a part of your scrapbooks. The more aware you are of the details around you, the better you'll be able to record them. Photographs, by the way, are just one kind of memory trigger, one place to start when pulling together your own personal story. I've found that if I think about scrapbooking my pictures, I become quickly overwhelmed. But, if I think "memory first" and work on preserving a memory here and a memory there—one at a time, using my photos as illustrations, I feel inspired, focused and very rewarded for my efforts.

If you think in terms of pictures and you took 30 at your birthday party last week, and you have eight rolls of undeveloped film from Christmas and 60 images from last month's trip to your mom's house (incidentally waiting to be uploaded from your new digital camera), and you have half a dozen of those photo-eating magnetic albums from your childhood and a box that you just inherited from your great aunt…well, you're just not going to feel like diving right in!

If on the other hand, you stop and consider how different your life is from that of your great aunt, and how much you love fresh raspberry jam and instant messaging your sister and getting together at your mom's and finding a great bargain and

walking in the woods, then you begin to think, "I could take a photo of…" or "I could make a scrapbook page about…" and magical, creative things start to happen. The "should dos" are replaced with "could dos" and you see that **The Big Picture** of your life is much more than your piles, boxes, files and drawers of photos. In chapter one and two, you'll get a chance to compile a fun tag book to remind you that there are many facets of life, from the extraordinary to the everyday, that are worth commemorating.

The second reason this book is called **The Big Picture** is because I'm going to share with you the context that we don't often see—the proverbial forest that gets lost for the trees. I'm often asked questions like these:

- *Do you have family albums for each year?*
- *If you go camping, do you make a page for each of your boys?*
- *Just how many theme albums do you have?*
- *If I were to make a page about my love of spicy Thai food, where would I put it?*

Scrapbook questions like these can boggle your mind. I hope you don't let that happen, because I've got solutions. I can't wait to tell you about some very liberating and simplifying ways to store and share your pages. **The Big Picture** in scrapbooking is much more than finished pages—

it's scrapbook albums. Ask yourself just a few questions; and you'll be able to determine how and where you want your scrapbooks to be enjoyed. With this vision in mind, confusion turns into clarity and you find answers perfectly suited to your situation.

There's one last reason this book is called **The Big Picture**, and it's the biggest of all. But there's no way I'm going to hand it over to you this early in the book; you'll just have to keep reading. Hang in there, because it's most definitely worth your time!

The Big Picture is ultimately my approach to scrapbooking. It's what I do, why I do it, and how it's altered my outlook and enhanced my perspective. I hope in this book you find page ideas you can use. I hope the projects spark your creativity. Most of all, I hope you have fun reading. I hope you can tell how much fun I have scrapbooking. I've let go of the obligation, the guilt, and the pressure to be anything but me. I've rewritten the rules and squashed unrealistic expectations. Scrapbooking makes me happy.

Get the picture?

Stacy

Nothing is too small to know, and nothing is too big to attempt.
WILLIAM VAN HORNE

how to use this book

CHAPTERS 1 AND 2
pages and projects

The first time through:

- Look at the layouts, theme albums and projects to get ideas.

- Read my journaling. Whether it's one line, or a full page—I've shared a bit of me, my life. Ask yourself how you could do the same. I don't expect grammatical perfection from myself, so I hope you won't either. What I lack in precision I make up for in authenticity—listen to my voice and use it to find your own.

On second and subsequent readings:

- Focus on my why, where and what. This is the behind-the-scenes stuff that we don't normally talk about in magazines and idea books, but it's the essence of what I most want to share—in a nutshell, the notion that it's not just the completed page that matters, but why you created it in the first place, how you intend to share it with others, and what you learned from the process.

Make a tag book:

- Tear the tag pages from the back and trim out each tag. Now, flip through the book again and look for the little tag icons—read each tag description and think about it. Complete the tags in whatever order you like. Please don't expect yourself to do this in one sitting, or even over the course of a few days. Give yourself time. Explore and experiment with your ideas. Listen to your intuition, jot notes and play a little. Be true to yourself and you'll begin to see your own big picture. This tag book will become your personal scrapbooking mission statement. It's a little reminder of life topics that you may otherwise overlook—an inspiration piece to guide you in realizing your potential as a photojournalist. To assemble them into a tag book, punch a hole in each tag and place them all on a jump ring or thread them onto a ribbon. Hang your book in your creative space and refer to it often.

Family Fun
Library

CHAPTER 3
other stuff

Big Picture Planning

Ask yourself these questions to help you plan for and create the albums that will best celebrate your unique life. A big-picture plan is like the list you take to the grocery store—you're free to deviate from it, but it will guide you so you don't forget the items you really need.

Stacy's Albums

I have several ongoing album systems, for lack of a better term, that have helped liberate me from the unrealistic expectations we all place on ourselves. I share them with you here.

Project Creativity

I believe that seeing yourself as a creative person and learning to nurture and express this inborn trait is absolutely essential to enriching your scrapbooks, and your life. These pages are all about impressing this on your mind and encouraging you to devote time and energy to the pursuit of creative thinking!

Information and Inspiration

This is simply a visual resource list of a few of my favorite books and websites, with the hope that you might enjoy learning from them also!

Materials Lists and Design Notes

They say life is in the details. So, here they are— a reference of the specific products I used on every page and project. A discussion of design is not the main purpose of this book, but internalizing a few key principles will guide your decisions and save you time. If you need help recognizing the influence of design, or just want a quick refresher, the notes are here!

Stacy's Tags

My tag book is here, so you can see how I've approached this fun project. Use your tags to discover and record your own scrapbook "touch points." Make your tag book a reflection of you!

Let's go!

If you pay attention at every moment, you form a new relationship to time. In some magical way, by slowing down, you become more efficient, productive, and energetic, focusing without distraction directly on the task in front of you. Not only do you become immersed in the moment, you become the moment.

MICHAEL RAY

pages

highlights 2004

WHY | Because I make a family highlight page at the end of every year. I make five color copies of these pages and exchange them with my parents and four siblings' families, for Christmas.

WHERE | In the *Christmas Exchange* album (page 111).

WHAT | This album has 48 layouts documenting the lives of my extended family. Okay, that's really cool. My boys call this their "cousins book," and they love looking through it when I pull it out each Christmas. I've learned over the last eight years that I'd much rather get a scrapbook page from my brother and his family than whatever else they might give me. I love the connection that I feel through these pages. They are a personal and meaningful gift.

At the beginning of each year, start a photo file, where you can store one photo from each season and major event. This will make assembling a highlights page very easy.

elmo

WHY | I walked into Taft's room one morning to find that he had dressed himself in his red sweat pants and a white turtleneck (he is my only boy who will wear turtlenecks, which I love). Anyway, I said to him, "Hey cutie boy, you match Elmo today," and then it happened. I got one of those little visions of a potential scrapbook page, and so I did what any good scrapbooker would do—grabbed my camera, combed my kid's hair, and propped some fun shots.

WHERE | In the *All About Us* album, behind the *Taft* tab.

WHAT | I love ordering photos at *Walmart.com*. I can upload half a dozen images, order them in any size I want, and pick them up in an hour. In the past, I rarely bothered to get enlargements—too much effort—but now, even lazy me can scrapbook 8 x 10s!

When you decide to do something to one side of a two-page layout, step back and ask yourself if you can do something similar to the other side. Orange circles on the left? How about an orange circle on the right? Think of it like balancing an equation in math. Its called repetition, and 9 times out of 10, it's the answer you need.

13

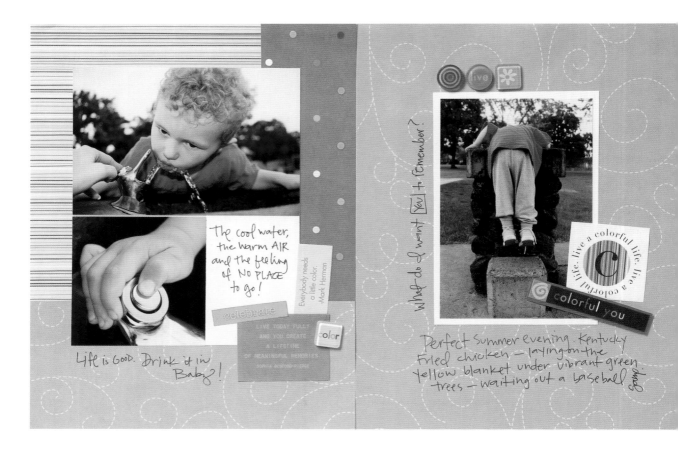

The cool water,
the warm AIR
and the feeling
of NO PLACE
to go!

Everybody needs
a little color.
Mark Herman

celebrate

color

LIVE TODAY FULLY
AND YOU CREATE
A LIFETIME
OF MEANINGFUL MEMORIES.
SOPHIA BEDFORD-PIERCE

Life is Good. Drink it in
Baby!

What do I want you to remember?

live

live a colorful life. live a colorful life.

C

colorful you

Perfect Summer evening. Kentucky
Fried chicken — laying on the
yellow blanket under vibrant green
trees — waiting out a baseball game.

colorful you

WHY | After a long week with too many phone meetings talking about scrapbooking, I needed to recharge and feel creative again. I tucked the kids into bed, hooked up to my iPod, and pulled out the coordinated line of paper called *Colorful*, by KI memories—'cause it made me happy. I then randomly selected one of my photo albums (where I store unscrapped photos) from the shelf and said, "I'll scrap the first photos that speak to me." This page is the result.

WHERE | In the *All About Us* album, behind the *Taft* tab.

WHAT | Staying up late doesn't always make you tired the next day. There are different ways to refuel; filling up my creative tank is like a great night's sleep to my soul. It's delightful to wake up to a fresh scrapbook page—is it as good this morning as I thought it was last night?

The next time you're in a craft or discount store, cruise by the floral aisle and pick up some inexpensive silk flowers. To use one on a page, pull the flower off the stem and then remove the center. Now use a brad to attach it to your layout!

Taft Sept '04

Am I supposed to say Don't pick the Flowers?

I don't think so.

flowers

WHY | I bought these cute silk flowers while running errands one afternoon. An enlarged version of this picture is displayed in my family room. At home, putting away the groceries, I unpacked the flowers, saw the picture, looked at the flowers, and then looked at the picture again. "I feel a page coming on!" I exclaimed. I've already used this photo in my *Photos I Love* album (page 110), but I wanted to use it again. (This, by the way, is perfectly okay!)

WHERE | In the *All About Us* album, behind the *Taft* tab.

WHAT | Scraplifting saves so much time. See page 57, top left, in *Clean and Simple Scrapbooking*. Cathy Zielske, the author, is a master of one-photo pages, so I knew I would find a jumpstart there. I created this page in 30 minutes, and that includes the time it took me to pull out my sewing machine and thread it!

stacy

WHY | I was asked to teach a scrapbooking class to 10- and 11-year-old girls at church. I wanted to teach them how important it is to scrapbook themselves, so I asked them questions like, "What are your favorite colors?" "How do you want people to describe you?" and "What is something you are really good at?" Their one or two word answers became the word-collage tag, to which they added two or three pictures of themselves. This is the "sample" page I created the night before.

WHERE | In the *All About Us* album, behind the Stacy tab.

WHAT | Girls are louder than you may think, especially when there are 16 of them with hammers. They are also extremely eager to do their own thing, which is healthy! They didn't compare their work with their neighbors. They also didn't stress over slight imperfections. Watching them reminded me to let my "inner-girl" come out to play!

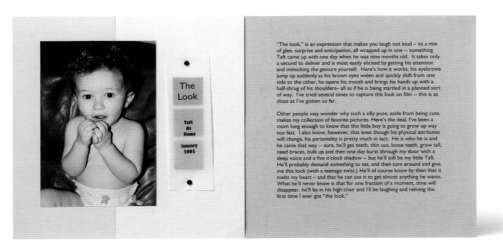

Text within photo:

The
Look

Taft
At
Home

January
2003

"The look," is an expression that makes you laugh out loud – its a mix of glee, surprise and anticipation, all wrapped up in one -- something Taft came up with one day when he was nine months old. It takes only a second to deliver and is most easily elicited by getting his attention and mimicking the gesture yourself. Here's how it works, his eyebrows jump up suddenly as his brown eyes widen and quickly shift from one side to the other, he opens his mouth and brings his hands up with a half-shrug of his shoulders– all as if he is being startled in a planned sort of way. I've tried several times to capture this look on film -- this is as close as I've gotten so far.

Other people may wonder why such a silly pose, aside from being cute, makes my collection of favorite pictures. Here's the deal, I've been a mom long enough to know that this little boy is going to grow up way too fast. I also know, however, that even though his physical attributes will change, his personality is pretty much in tact. He is who he is and he came that way -- sure, he'll get teeth, thin out, loose teeth, grow tall, need braces, bulk up and then one day burst through my door with a deep voice and a five o'clock shadow -- but he'll still be my little Taft. He'll probably demand something to eat, and then turn around and give me this look (with a teenage twist.) He'll of course know by then that it melts my heart – and that he can use it to get almost anything he wants. What he'll never know is that for one fraction of a moment, time will disappear, he'll be in his high chair and I'll be laughing and reliving the first time I ever got "the look."

the look

W H Y | Because I knew I wanted to capture this expression that has become "so Taft."

W H E R E | In my *Photos I Love* album (page 110).

W H A T | Sitting down to write how a photo makes you feel, or what you see in it, isn't easy. It takes time. I've simplified the design of this album so that I will take the time to write. I usually have to do this kind of writing late at night, when the house is still. I rarely show finished scrapbook pages to my husband, but for some reason I always read him the entries in my *Photos I Love* album.

so different

W H Y | I was looking for a particular photo in my chronological storage albums and came across this photo of Chase. I thought, "That is so Chase!" and I pulled it to put in his personality file. Two minutes later I found the photo of Trey, and a minute after that, the photo of Clark. Still searching for the original photo, I began reflecting on my children, their personalities, and how very different they are. That's when the idea hit me. I quickly found a Taft personality picture, jumped up and made this page. I still can't find that other photo. In fact, now I don't even remember what it was I was looking for.

W H E R E | I don't know yet. I may actually put it in one of those acrylic page frames and hang it on the door to the basement.

so different

W H A T | Not to worry so much about page size. Most of my pages are 8½ x 11, but when it feels right, I use 12 x 12. There are so many things we stress about; page size shouldn't be one of them.

So, there I was wandering around Barnes and Noble, browsing the new titles table, when I pick up this book and hear myself say, "That's right, he's dead." And then without any warning at all, I start to cry — I mean I guess I knew I liked Mr. Rogers, but why the sudden emotion? Why now, as an almost 40 year-old woman am I completely caught off guard. I turn the book over, and there pictured on the back cover are the blue sneakers – now, I'm doing that laugh, cry thing and I'm starting to draw undue attention to myself. As I flip through the pages I begin to silently sing "*It's such a good feeling to know you're alive, it's such a happy feeling you're growing inside …* I can't believe I know all the words … *I think I'll start a snappy new day …* I guess my childhood wasn't that long ago, because suddenly I see Trolley come through the tunnel and I see all my make-believe friends; King Friday, Prince Tuesday, Meow, Meow Kitty, X the Owl, and that weird Elaine lady in the round house. Lady Aberlin and Mr. McFeely – they're all there, in my mind's eye. I can so remember feeding the fish and watching the magical picture come to life –it would take me to cool places, like factories where crayons and paper are made. Wow, Who knew – I guess one person really can make a difference. In a world that is often cruel and crass, it's nice to know there a people like Fred Rogers – decent, kind and unhurried. So, Mr. Rogers – here's to you. Thank you. Maybe, just maybe if I live a good life I will someday get to be your neighbor.

people tag

Who are the people you work with, sing in the church choir with or play bunco with? Who do you admire, in your immediate circle of acquaintances, in pop culture or in world history? Other people are important characters in our stories. So whether it's your daughter's ballet teacher or your favorite newspaper columnist, their names go here so you can think about how to include them in your scrapbooks.

mr. rogers

WHY | Okay, this is a bit weird, but when I saw this book in Barnes and Noble, I picked it up, read the back cover and started to get really emotional— a sign I took as evidence that I needed to pay tribute to my fondness for Fred Rogers and his long-running PBS show.

WHERE | I suppose it could go in the *All About Us* album, behind the *Stacy* tab, since it describes my emotional tendencies, but I'm going to put it in *People We Love* album, behind the *Friends* tab— I think good neighbors belong there!

WHAT | I like how it felt to respond to an emotional moment like I had in the bookstore. Creating this page validated that emotion and gave it a permanent place to live. I'm learning to embrace my sensitivity—it still bugs me when I cry in a business meeting, but it's who I am.

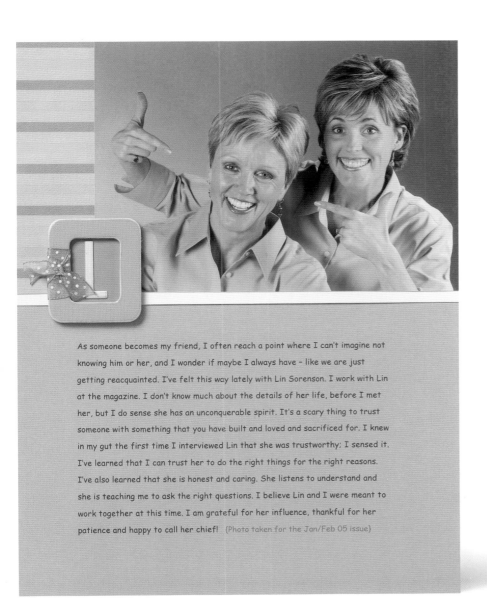

As someone becomes my friend, I often reach a point where I can't imagine not knowing him or her, and I wonder if maybe I always have – like we are just getting reacquainted. I've felt this way lately with Lin Sorenson. I work with Lin at the magazine. I don't know much about the details of her life, before I met her, but I do sense she has an unconquerable spirit. It's a scary thing to trust someone with something that you have built and loved and sacrificed for. I knew in my gut the first time I interviewed Lin that she was trustworthy; I sensed it. I've learned that I can trust her to do the right things for the right reasons. I've also learned that she is honest and caring. She listens to understand and she is teaching me to ask the right questions. I believe Lin and I were meant to work together at this time. I am grateful for her influence, thankful for her patience and happy to call her chief! {Photo taken for the Jan/Feb 05 issue}

lin

WHY | I pretty much said it in my journaling. Basically, life changes and you never know when you're going to meet someone who will become such a part of you that you can't imagine it any other way. I love the pic—it reminds me of a happy day surrounded by my team, taking goofy magazine head shots.

WHERE | In the *People We Love* album, behind the *Friends* tab.

WHAT | I made this page in about 10 minutes, but then I put the little wood frame on and took it off and put it on and took it off. I gotta hope I'm not the only one who does this? I'm thinking now maybe I should have left if off. Oh well, next page.

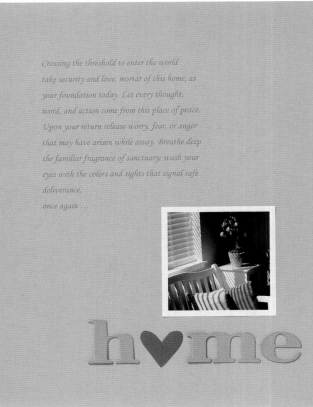

home

W H Y | My home isn't perfect and I have a "someday" list a mile long, but every now and then, when I see it in the right light, I stop and I realize that where we live right now is where my most treasured memories reside. Home isn't the weathered park bench retrieved from the patio, the build-it-yourself furniture, or the stained slipcovers and carpet; home is a safe haven for the people inside. That's reason enough.

W H E R E | I haven't done it yet, but I'm going to find an album and create a title page that says *There's No Place Like Home*. In the meantime, this page goes in the *Places We Go* album, behind the *Home* tab I added recently.

W H A T | I'm a believer in personal journaling, but sometimes the words of a quote or a poem say exactly what you feel. In these cases, I have learned to let the words speak, uncluttered.

home tag

Can you walk into your girlfriend's kitchen and make a sandwich? Does Grandma still have cards you made her in the upstairs bedroom? Home is not just your current address. Home is where you feel safe, where you let down your guard. Where is home for you? Jot down these safe places on this tag—you might use the back to add one specific memory you have from each of these "homes."

homemaker

WHY | I wish I had pictures of the living room in my childhood home. My mother patched together pieces of shag carpet from the dumpster behind the carpet store, built her own bookshelf, and hung her own jungle-print wallpaper. I had no idea how resourceful she was. I just danced to my Burl Ives record there, played Für Elise on the piano there, and watched hours upon hours of Beaver and Gilligan there. It was a happy place.

WHERE | In my future *Home* album—did I mention I want to intersperse layouts with full-page quotes? I just found an inspirational little book called *House Blessings,* by June Cotner, that I love!

WHAT | This layout and the previous one were originally intended to be a two-page spread, but as I played with the pieces, the idea of a separate *Home* and *Homemaker* layout emerged. I love the power that I wield over my home. Call me domestic goddess, queen bee, or director of the interior; I can set, alter, or completely change the mood in my home—most often with my attitude, and every other year or so, with a can of paint. Don't be so set on the outcome of a layout that you miss a chance to be inspired.

I could tell you
that I love
Wendy because
she is incredibly
bright, resourceful
and nurturing—
or you could
just read
← this!

WHY Are you
so good
to me?

An email
exchange 3.15

my friend Wendy

wendy

WHY | Because I adore my friend Wendy. She's the most nurturing human being I have ever encountered. She sent me an e-mail last March with a dozen or more websites that I could visit for inspiration in writing this book. I printed out her message and then replied, "Why are you so good to me?" She responded, "Because you make me laugh and you are my friend, and you bought me my first pair of fuzzy socks."

WHERE | In the *People We Love* album, behind the *Friends* tab.

WHAT | We can do so much more to celebrate the friendships we value. Letters, e-mail, and even messages on your answering machine can become journaling that describes a special friendship.

Give your page a "fresh" aged look. Run a sponge brush dipped in white acrylic paint along the edge of papers, photos and accents.

from forty to five

WHY | This page started out as a tribute to my love of ribbon, and I set out to find a photo of "little me" with a ribbon in my hair. But the longer I stared at the photo, the more I knew I wanted to write about something else. I ended up with a version of the "all I ever needed to know I learned in kindergarten" idea. When you think about it, it's remarkable what we know at such a young age. Try writing a letter to your younger self and see what you learn.

WHERE | In the *All About Us* album, behind the *Stacy* tab.

WHAT | There is almost always a way to add more journaling to your pages. In this case, I turned the original journaling block into a pocket to hold additional tags.

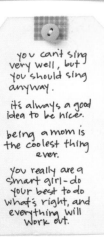

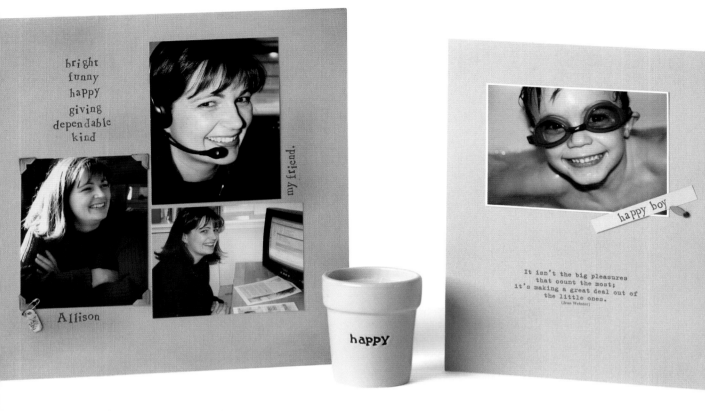

my friend allison

WHY | I found this adorable little candle at Target and let it inspire me. The colors reminded me of Allison, so I went to my *Stacy Friends* photo file to find photos of her. The page was done in 15 minutes. (I was having so much fun that I created the *Happy Boy* layout, too!)

WHERE | The *Allison* page has been in a pile with other homeless 12 x 12 layouts. I think I'm going to put them all in a big black album and make a title page that says *Just Because*. I want to put an index at the back that shares why I made each page. (*Happy Boy* goes in the *All About Us* album, behind the *Trey* tab).

WHAT | Target is my all-time favorite store, and if my house ever burns down, I'm moving in. Of course I already knew that. (Yes, I've done a *Target* layout—it's on page 54.)

We think you need to improve your road rage score.

maple syrup balloons? cool.

bedtime? Not 'til you've read two comic books and watched some pro wrestling.

why not drink it straight from the milk carton?

Great rap song. Turn it louder so we can all hear?

why don't you control the remote? you have better taste than your brother?

Stick your arms out of the car window— there's a breeze!

o.k. — but don't let homework cut into your TV time.

No point in making the bed when you'll just have to unmake it.

No — we're not there yet, but please keep asking!

2005

chase— I've never seen you laugh so hard as when you read this to me. funny boy !?

From "this book's a joke." [your favorite] read.

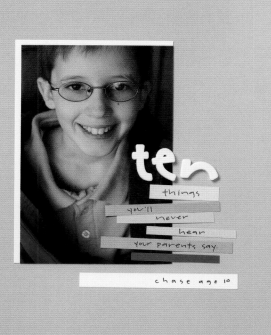

ten things you'll never hear your parents say.

chase age 10

ten

W H Y | Because Chase came to me not long ago laughing so hard he could barely breathe. "Mom," he said, "I'm going to read you something from *This Book's A Joke*—just don't be mad, okay?" He proceeded to read me "Ten Things You'll Never Hear Your Parents Say." I knew I needed to document Chase and his sense of humor. It's so much a part of his personality at ten.

W H E R E | In the *All About Us* album, behind the *Chase* tab.

W H A T | Anything can inspire a scrapbook page, and the more you open yourself up, the more you will find to inspire you. Go to *oopsimeantto.com* to see the inspiration for this page.

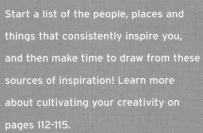

inspiration tag

Start a list of the people, places and things that consistently inspire you, and then make time to draw from these sources of inspiration! Learn more about cultivating your creativity on pages 112-115.

chill-dren

WHY | I made this page for one of my classes at Creating Keepsakes University. My goal was to encourage students to be more "flexible" with their scrapbooking routine. I suggested they use a color combination that is opposite of what you would consider normal or expected—hence a "green" snow page. I then challenged them to use the same product on another layout (see next page).

WHERE | I don't know. I created it with my class in mind, not my scrapbooks. I'll figure it out sooner or later.

WHAT | I almost always love having a deadline. How could you create a deadline to encourage some quick decision-making and finished pages?

i love growing things

WHY | Since I knew I was working with green, I went looking for "green" pictures. Garden photos were perfect!

WHERE | I'm putting this one in the *Things We Do* album, behind the *Accomplishments* tab, because I think growing beautiful green beans and healthy boys is worth some kudos.

WHAT | I love paper strips. They are a trusted paper treatment of mine. You can cut them thick or thin and they're always "in"—hey, cute rhyme.

The next time you finish a page and have product spread out all over your scrap space, make another page. While you're at it, make a card or two! I like having a stockpile of generic cards made up. This is a huge time-saver for me!

Note to Self - enlarge This one!

Chase Taft Trey

Pull 4.

Summer 2004

To set up your own color organizers, you'll need ten shallow drawers or bins, one each for reds, pinks, oranges, yellows, greens, blues, purples, browns, whites and (whew) gray and black, together. As you purchase generic accents and embellishments, break them up and store them in your drawers.

chase, trey, taft

WHY | I had my camera on portrait mode when I took this picture. It turns out that's what I should have done, but I didn't know that because I'd never read the manual! I love the result. I never want to forget these faces. Pictures like this happen so rarely at my house that when I get one it's scrapbook time for sure. I know photo shoots are nice, but I still think the best shots are those candid, it-happened-one-afternoon-in-the-park, stroke-of-pure-luck kinds. They are so real. The pull tab says "3 of the 4 cutest and most charming children on the face of the planet." Any questions?"

WHERE | Remember the big, black *Just Because* album? This one goes there too.

WHAT | I love, love, love my color drawers! For me, they are much more than an organizational solution. I generally begin a layout by pulling cardstock and/or patterned papers I want to use, and playing with photo placement. At this point, I can pull out one or two of my color drawers (like orange and green) and let myself play! Almost without exception, I end up using embellishments that I would not have initially considered. This is exceptionally good for my creativity.

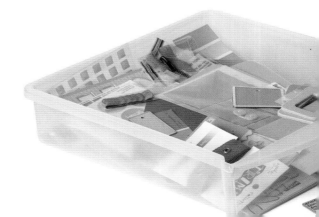

school shopping 2004

WHY | School shopping day is a tradition in our family. Every year in August, each boy gets one day with mom to acquire the new clothes and supplies needed for the coming year. Lunch and a treat are included. I hadn't yet made a page for Chase about this annual event.

WHERE | In the *Things We Do* album, behind the *Traditions* tab.

Put items like buttons and brads into small, clear containers before placing them in your drawers.

WHAT | Just because you do it once a year does not mean you must scrapbook it every year! I don't scrapbook annual events annually, unless there is a compelling reason to do so. As soon as I made this decision, I felt 20 pounds of obligation—which, by the way, is the early stage of guilt—fall away.

Remember: You can change your approach any time you need to. Even if you've done something a certain way for a number of years, you can change. This wonderful hobby needs to work for you—not the other way around.

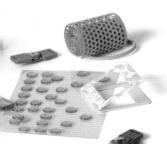

my favorite source of inspiration

I've always ♡'d magazines, but I could have never guessed how acutely aware I would become...

I subscribe, I buy I study, I learn I mark pages, tear out ideas, compare cover lines and stare at newstands I count ads and critique design and it fascinates me.

So... everytime we walk into Walmart, Albertsons, Barnes and Noble or Target the boys say "Mom- want me to go move your magazine to the front?" — Well trained eh?

Did you know... There are 3,500-4,000 companies publishing approx. 12,000 magazines? Wow!

mag mania

W H Y | Because never in a million years did I dream I would be involved with the production of a magazine! Now, I'm often more aware than I want to be. I will intentionally choose the longest line at the supermarket, so I have more time to study magazine covers, cover-lines, mastheads and contents pages—all stuff I didn't know a thing about five years ago.

W H E R E | In the *All About Us* album, behind the *Stacy* tab.

W H A T | I'm really enjoying the texture that the "bits and pieces" of my world bring to my pages. Start a little file of "cultural" memorabilia: stuff like tags from clothing, an occasional receipt, boarding passes (see next page), postage stamps, maybe the nutrition label from your favorite candy bar. It's all a part of your life.

culture tag

Think about the activities, philosophies and behaviors that describe your life in the 21st century. Where do you work? What do you do there? How would you describe your community? Where and how do you buy the things you need? What role does the media, modern science and technology play in your life? All this and more contribute to your "culture" and much of it will change in your lifetime. Include these kinds of bits and pieces in your story!

You know you travel too much when ...

- You have a favorite stall in your airport bathroom.
- You know your TSA agents by name.
- You receive pink booties from SWA for Valentine's Day.
- All of the books on your nightstand have boarding passes for bookmarks.
- You have an "airplane" playlist on your i-pod.
- You've taken your husband and four children to Disney World on frequent flyer miles!
- Your mother calls your cell and instead of saying "Hi honey, how are you?" she says "Hi honey, where are you?"

fly girl

WHY | Because as much as I'd like to believe I'm a homebody, I travel quite a bit for my job with the magazine. I've been saving odd pieces of airplane memorabilia for a while, so when the idea of a humorous (but true) list proving my frequent flyer status presented itself, everything fell into place.

WHERE | In the *All About Us* album, behind the *Stacy* tab.

WHAT | "Fill-in-the-blank" journaling starters are great. The one I used on this page is a favorite of mine: You know_____ (fill in some words here) when _____ (create a list here.) Example: You know you travel too much when: (followed by a list.) Sometimes all you need is the first sentence and then the rest will come.

I love you

WHY | If you haven't heard the *Bushel and a Peck* song, you really should Google it, because it's such a darn cute song. I grew up singing this song in the car, and I now sing it to my boys. A couple of years ago, I burned a bunch of songs from my childhood onto a CD for my siblings, and they all loved it. This should say something about the memories tied up in music.

WHERE | In our *Sing-along* album (page 111).

WHAT | Everyday snapshots and duplicates—what I call left-over pictures—are perfect illustrations for pages like this. Here are eight pictures, taken at eight different times, from 1998 to 2004, from Christmas morning to Father's Day, to my anniversary and in between. Give yourself permission to mix it up a little!

i've been thinking about...
pictures

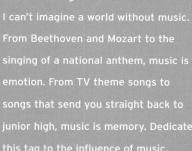

He is

WHY | Because songwriter and vocalist Hilary Weeks is my favorite when it comes to inspirational music. I find this particular song very moving. When I stop to think about it, what I most want to give my children is a foundation of faith. I want them to be good, God-fearing men. I think music will help me do this and I also think there should be evidence of this faith-promoting music in my scrapbooks.

WHERE | One of the albums I'm starting in 2005 is a *Faithbook*. I will use a rich, brown leather album that I intend to display with other books in our living room.

WHAT | I enjoyed searching for photos that visually represent the words of this song and the feelings it stirs in me—photographic evidence of a blessed life. Take this approach with your photos just once and you'll begin to sense the power you have to create something truly meaningful.

music tag

I can't imagine a world without music. From Beethoven and Mozart to the singing of a national anthem, music is emotion. From TV theme songs to songs that send you straight back to junior high, music is memory. Dedicate this tag to the influence of music, musicians, and the songs that make you want to sing, dance or even clean!

CHASE'S GIFT

A natural inclination to love and lift others — something that takes others a life of service to achieve — you are a gift, my son.

He's not heavy — he's my brother.

chase's gift

WHY | Chase has ADHD. This means that when it comes to measuring his success by many of our society's standards, he falls short. It is my privilege as his mother to celebrate his unique talents and abilities—those that might otherwise go unnoticed. I love that scrapbooking allows me to do this in such a tangible way.

WHERE | In the *All About Us* album, behind the *Chase* tab.

WHAT | You really don't have to write about the pictures themselves. Dates and places are great historical tidbits, but they don't describe people. When I look through my grandfather's well-documented photo album, I wish it included details about the people!

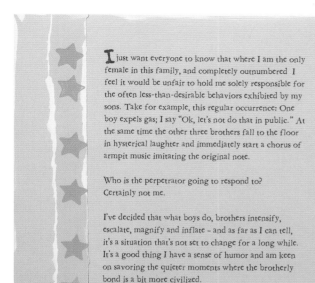

I just want everyone to know that where I am the only female in this family, and completely outnumbered I feel it would be unfair to hold me solely responsible for the often less-than-desirable behaviors exhibited by my sons. Take for example, this regular occurrence: One boy expels gas; I say "Ok, let's not do that in public." At the same time the other three brothers fall to the floor in hysterical laughter and immediately start a chorus of armpit music imitating the original note.

Who is the perpetrator going to respond to? Certainly not me.

I've decided that what boys do, brothers intensify, escalate, magnify and inflate – and as far as I can tell, it's a situation that's not set to change for a long while. It's a good thing I have a sense of humor and am keen on savoring the quieter moments where the brotherly bond is a bit more civilized.

Boys and Brothers – what a combination!

boys and brothers

WHY | I feel a regular need to scrapbook the relationship of four boys in my home; the brotherly bond is so unique. One minute they're pounding on each other and the next they're all snuggled up under a blanket fort watching a movie. I try to savor the chaos, knowing that all too soon I'll have the quiet I yearn for. I often feel very alone in my femaleness, but hey, at least I'm not bored!

WHERE | In the *All About Us* album, behind the *Oh Brother* tab.

WHAT | I love how inexpensive it is to get great big pictures. I think I already said that, but now that the whole idea of an enlargement isn't that "special" I'm giving myself the chance to play and try new things. I'm certainly not on the cutting edge of techniques, but I painted and stamped right on my photo—how cool is that?

Put up your "relationship radar" and start taking more photos of people interacting. Pages that capture human relationships are priceless.

favorite fourth of july memories

WHY | Because for years, parts and pieces of my extended family have gathered at various places on the 4th of July. Post 9/11, these gatherings that celebrate family and freedom have been especially savored. I've noticed details and participated with a child-like enthusiasm. Swells of love and patriotism are more common, and I like that.

WHERE | I'm going to put it in our *Family Celebrations* album (page 110), behind the *Reunions* tab. That's really what these gatherings are—unofficial reunions.

WHAT | If you've been scrapbooking long, you probably know which products are "new" and which are not. Guess what? Your family doesn't know—and better yet, they don't care. Use what you have. It's all good! Scrapbooking products don't have an expiration date. Remind yourself of this often.

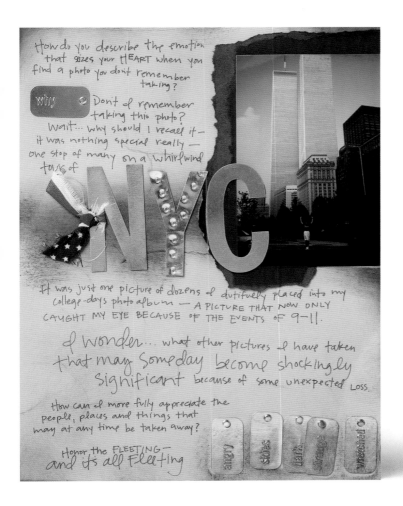

How do you describe the emotion that sizes your HEART when you find a photo you don't remember taking?

why ● Don't I remember taking this photo? Wait... why should I recall it — it was nothing special really — one stop of many on a whirlwind tour of

NYC

It was just one picture of dozens I dutifully placed into my college-days photo album — A PICTURE THAT NOW ONLY CAUGHT MY EYE BECAUSE OF THE EVENTS OF 9-11.

I wonder... what other pictures I have taken that may someday become shockingly significant because of some unexpected loss.

How can I more fully appreciate the people, places and things that may at any time be taken away?

Honor the FLEETING — and it's all Fleeting

angry   skies   dark   strange   wretched

The colors and techniques you use should reflect the emotion you feel. Juvenile accents capture carefree holiday moments, while distressed grays and metallic accents speak to the cold, dark feelings of loss. Pause and think about the emotion before you pull out papers and accents. Then select materials accordingly.

nyc

WHY | I recently came across this photo from my college days and it completely caught me off-guard. I don't even remember visiting the World Trade Center! I took it upstairs to show my husband and it sat on my nightstand for several weeks until I felt ready to write about it. I didn't pre-write the journaling because I didn't want it finessed—I just wanted the questions and ideas to roll off my brain.

I have a little bin full of metal dog-tag accents and they seemed a natural choice after I selected the large metal letters for NYC. It was shocking to me that I randomly pulled such an interesting combination of tags from my bin—just these: 'angry,' 'skies,' 'dark,' 'strange,' 'wretched' and 'why.' Sometimes everything seems to just come together when you're scrapbooking!

WHERE | I'm not sure yet. (This is okay!) Just remember you don't create something because you have a place for it to go. You create because you feel compelled to do so.

WHAT | The value of a photograph can change. Take some time to look back through older photos. Are there any that have taken on new meaning, since you last saw them? Consider recording your insights.

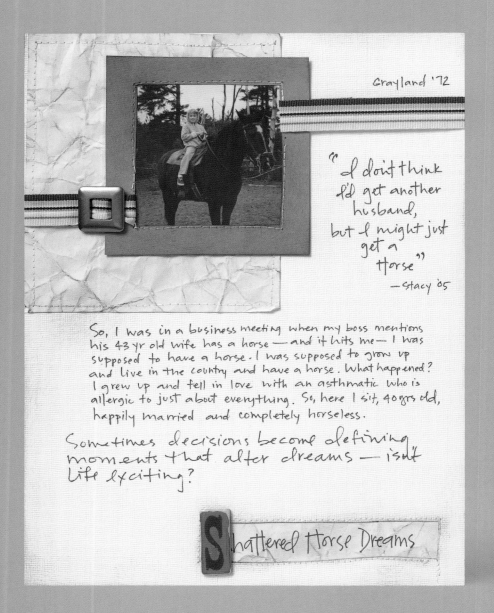

Grayland '72

" I don't think
I'd get another
husband,
but I might just
get a
Horse "
—Stacy '05

So, I was in a business meeting when my boss mentions
his 43 yr old wife has a horse — and it hits me — I was
supposed to have a horse. I was supposed to grow up
and live in the country and have a horse. What happened?
I grew up and fell in love with an asthmatic who is
allergic to just about everything. So, here I sit, 40 yrs old,
happily married and completely horseless.

Sometimes decisions become defining
moments that alter dreams — isn't
life exciting?

Shattered Horse Dreams

shattered horse dreams

WHY | This is a true "moments" page, as it records the moment I became fully conscious of the fact that my little-girl dreams of owning a horse were not to be. I immediately thought of a vacation to the ocean, when we rode horses along the beach. I found this photo in my crumbling childhood scrapbook and gave it a new home.

WHERE | Right now, this page goes in the *All About Us* album, behind the *Stacy* tab, but I think I may pull several layouts like this together and put them in an album called *The Girl I Was, and the*

Woman I Am: Reflections and Random Memories. It will be a place for the very ordinary and strangely related things I remember.

WHAT | I'm finding that I'm incorporating many of my childhood photos into my current scrapbooks, as I discover connections. The freedom I have given myself to do this is allowing me to tell a richer story of me. I really didn't have a visual in my mind for this page, so I turned to Rebecca Sower's work for inspiration. I have always been amazed at her ability to bring childhood photos to life.

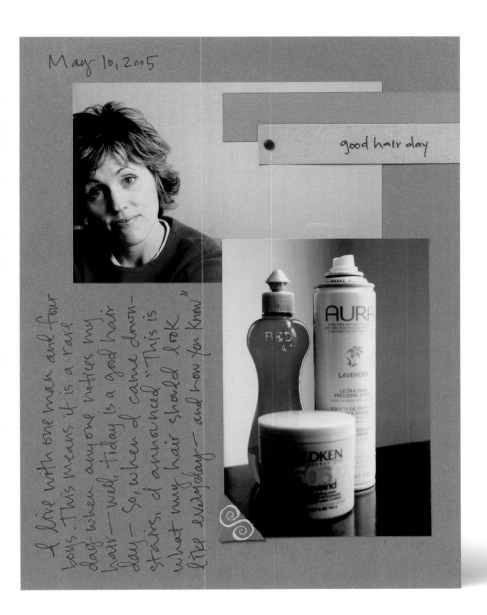

May 10, 2005

good hair day

I live with one man and four boys. This means it is a rare day when anyone notices my hair—well, today is a good hair day—So, when I came down-stairs, I announced "This is what my hair should look like everyday—and now you know"

Every time I walk by a paint display in a store, I stop and pick out two or three paint-chip combination cards, like the ones below, to inspire me. It's like free color advice from expert designers. If you like the results, punch a hole in the card and keep them on a jump ring in your creative space.

good hair day

W H Y | My hair looked really good, what can I say? If we can't use scrapbooking to capture these exceptionally important aspects of our life then what is it for?

W H E R E | In the *All About Us* album, behind the *Stacy* tab.

W H A T | Sometimes I just start writing and when I run out of room, I'm done. Journaling doesn't always have to be "composed." Just write.

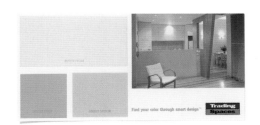

One night on my mission my companion and I were awakened by the sound of running water. Our apartment was flooding. Before I was fully alert, I had grabbed my scriptures and jumped onto my bed. I remember thinking "I could replace everything else, but I would be really sad if I lost my much-loved and well-marked scriptures. As my life has become more and more hectic I've learned to depend on my daily devotional, which isn't near as formal as it sounds. There is strength to be drawn from the silence of early morning and I need that. There really isn't much that can derail me when I start my day with prayer and scripture study.

But lay up for yourselves treasures in heaven, where neither moth nor rust doth corrupt, and where thieves do not break through nor steal: For where your treasure is, There will your heart be also.
Matthew 6:20-21

Recorded in this little book are some of my most favorite verses

treasure

WHY | Because I love reading from the scriptures. I've struggled to make regular study a part of my daily routine, and I'm happy to report that I've finally succeeded. If you love it, you've made time for it, and you've felt the rewards for this effort, it ought to be a part of your scrapbook.

WHERE | In the *All About Us* album, behind the *Stacy* tab.

WHAT | You don't always need an obvious title for every page you create. If it doesn't come, don't worry about it. It wasn't until I was completely finished with this page and looking for an accent to place in the mini-album window that the word-pebble became my title.

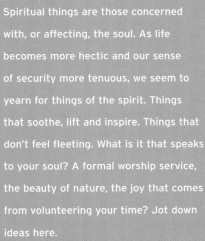

When I was fourteen or fifteen years old I ran into my parents room one night (probably to use my mom s hairspray or something.) My dad was kneeling by his bed praying . I don t remember what I thought in that moment, but I do know that the image of him on his knees has remained with me until this day. I don t remember my father ever giving me a sermon, and believe it or not, I don t remember ever being tempted to go against his will. He made me mad from time to time, but the thought of disappointing him even in a small way was too painful to consider. Now that I m a parent, I ve tried to figure out what it was exactly that my dad did. How did he inspire such compliance? The answer is integrity. There is no hypocrisy or dishonesty in him. He is an example of what he believes, 24/7. There is a scripture in the Book of Mormon that speaks of Captain Moroni. I think it suits my father as well.

If all men had been, and were, and ever would be, like unto Moroni, behold the very powers of hell would have been shaken forever, yea, the devil would never have power of the hearts of the children of men.

I pray I can teach my sons to be like my father.

integrity example

WHY | I took this picture of my father a couple of years ago, during the holidays, and have since wanted to use it all alone on a page. I really like the way he is sitting and the look in his eyes. This is my dad. During my morning run one day, something reminded me of him and I had a sudden swell of emotion and gratitude. The memory I wrote about came rushing back, and I knew I finally had my page!

WHERE | In the *People We Love* album, behind the *Grandparents* tab.

WHAT | Creating this page helped me realize that one of the things I love most about my father is that he is very spiritual without being pious. He doesn't criticize or gossip or judge anyone. I don't know that I would have been able to verbalize that before. Once again, scrapbooking has brought clarity!

spirituality tag

Spiritual things are those concerned with, or affecting, the soul. As life becomes more hectic and our sense of security more tenuous, we seem to yearn for things of the spirit. Things that soothe, lift and inspire. Things that don't feel fleeting. What is it that speaks to your soul? A formal worship service, the beauty of nature, the joy that comes from volunteering your time? Jot down ideas here.

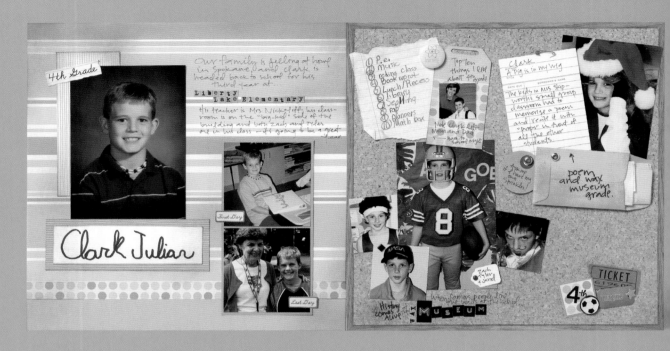

clark, 4th grade

WHY | I create five pages for each of my children at the end of each school year. These are the first two pages for Clark's 4th grade year. I try to use colors and accents that reflect the age and interests of that year.

WHERE | In Clark's *School of Life* album. Read more about this super-liberating approach to scrapbooking kids on pages 108-109.

WHAT | Honestly, we worry too much about scrapbooking all the pictures, events, holidays, milestones, etc. for our kids. All they really need are the highlights. My boys love their *School of Life* albums. These albums will be theirs to take with them when they are grown. The rest are mine. I guess they'll just have to come for a visit.

DISCO

does the dishes! It's true—when dinner's done and I've been deserted in the kitchen, feeling completely drained—I turn on the tunes. A good dose of Earth, Wind and Fire, KC or ABBA is all I need. I become a dancin' queen and a cleaning dynamo—dishes done.

disco does the dishes

W H Y | As my life has gotten busier, I've become acutely aware of what I call "coping strategies." They're things I do to energize myself and move past unpleasant or mundane duties that can bog down my daily life. Dancing to disco in the kitchen is one of those strategies. You'd be surprised how fast you can unload and load a dishwasher with Diana Ross as your back-up.

W H E R E | In the *All About Us* album, behind the *Stacy* tab.

W H A T | Unless you're one of the lucky few who live with a photography buff or scrapbooker, it's unlikely anyone will offer to take pictures of you. Get over it. Ask someone to take your picture when you want it. You may have to arrange for some uncomfortable photo shoots to capture the authentic (in my case, extremely nerdy) you, but you are worth the effort.

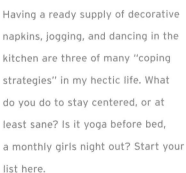

rituals tag

Having a ready supply of decorative napkins, jogging, and dancing in the kitchen are three of many "coping strategies" in my hectic life. What do you do to stay centered, or at least sane? Is it yoga before bed, a monthly girls night out? Start your list here.

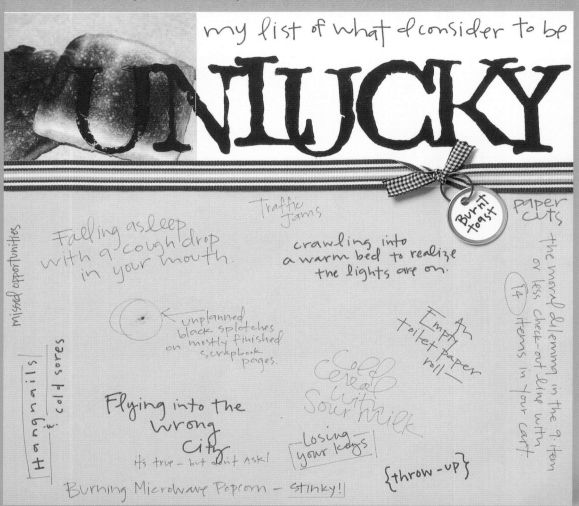

O.K.

my list of what I consider to be

UNLUCKY

Burnt toast

paper cuts

Traffic Jams

Falling asleep with a cough drop in your mouth.

crawling into a warm bed to realize the lights are on.

missed opportunities

The moral dilemma in the 9 item or less check-out line with 14 items in your cart

unplanned black splotches on mostly finished scrapbook pages.

Empty toilet paper roll

Hangnails

cold sores

Cold cereal with Sour Milk

Flying into the wrong City

It's true - but don't ASK!

losing your keys

{throw-up}

Burning Microwave Popcorn - Stinky!!

unlucky

WHY | I really like my son Clark's soccer coach. He never criticizes the players from the sidelines; instead, when he observes a missed opportunity he says in a booming voice "unlucky." He may say "unlucky" 20-plus times during the course of one game. His ability to react with restraint under pressure inspired this page. There's no sense in losing your cool—just call it unlucky.

WHERE | In the *Just Because* album—hey, this album is filling up fast!

WHAT | You know what's interesting? Most of the things on my unlucky list weren't even available to my great-grandmother. In other words, it's generally modern conveniences that inconvenience me. I wonder what my great-grandmother found unlucky about her life? She certainly didn't have car keys to lose or a microwave to burn popcorn in. And, do you know what would be truly unlucky? You and me not taking the chance to scrapbook these kinds of realizations and connections.

The 3 stars...

Now that's a **costume**

I don't remember who's idea this family get-up was, but I do recall the anticipation and cooperation that went into it. I found the Snow White costume on e-bay, Darci bought the

halloween 2003

beards, Grandpa made the cardboard picks and Grandma designed the hats and the handsome prince charming! Oh yeah, I suppose Clark gets some credit too — he shaved his head!

The 7 dwarfs...

Grandpa as Grumpy
Geof as Sneezy
Stacy as Doc
Clark as Dopey
Chase as Sleepy
Taft as Bashful
Ty as Happy

halloween 2003

WHY | In my opinion, Halloween is not about the candy, it's about the costumes! Halloween is a chance to "come as you aren't," and in our family, we take this challenge seriously. You should have seen the looks we got at the mall as our 10-person entourage made its way to the photo studio!

WHERE | In our *Halloween* album. This album comes out with the Halloween decorations. I just leave it out in the family room during the month of October! Do you have any idea how much fun it is to watch my boys grow up in just a few "costume" pages?

WHAT | Want to make a page really fast? Grab some pre-made product and a few photos, add some handwritten journaling and call it done. Choosing to do some pages quickly will allow time for the occasional masterpiece.

Don't forget you can alter, distress, or cut up paper and accents to make them work for you. Anytime you hear yourself say "I wish I had..." look around and say "What if I..." More often than not, I'm able to cut up, substitute, or even invent something I need.

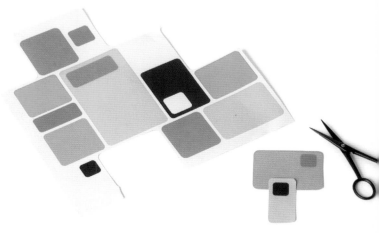

persistence of yellow

WHY | Because it was my favorite color when I was four years old, and it was still my favorite color when my mom and I decorated my bedroom at twelve. When I left home for college, I made a yellow bedspread to take with me. When we bought our first home, an interior decorator told me yellow was too warm for my south-facing kitchen. I ignored her advice, and bought a can of yellow paint. For these reasons and all the others that have caused the "persistence" of yellow in my life.

WHERE | I don't know, maybe I'll put it in the *Just Because* album.

WHAT | We are much more connected to color than we think, and we don't notice it enough. It feels good to identify with time-honored things— like your favorite color!

If part of a design works for you once, do it again! Notice the similarity between this layout and the one on page 46.

to your own observation, you may underestimate the significance of this photo. Please notice the hand that holds the pencil.

It seems lately
that nothing pleases
Geoffrey G. like
Geoffrey T.

left

WHY | I came upstairs on a Saturday afternoon to find Geof at the table doing preschool math with Taft. He looked up at me and whispered, "Look at this." I responded, "He's doing math!" "No," said Geof, "Look at this." He motioned towards Taft's left hand. The sparkle in dad's eye was reason alone to grab the camera.

WHERE | Initially, I thought this belonged in the *All About Us* album, behind the *Taft* tab, but Geof has far fewer pages in his section, so I think I'll put it there.

WHAT | Lengthy journaling is often laborious to read, even when it's well written. I like a less-is-more approach these days; I write it all down and then go back and zap the sentences I don't really need. When carefully selected words accompany a telling photo, it's easy to read between the lines.

Ahh.. my sweet chocolate, what can I say that would express my deep and undying affection for you? I love you. There are simply times, when you are the only thing that can make me feel better. You always seem to know exactly what I need, whether it's crunchy, smooth, dark, or cold and creamy — you are there when I need you most. I have a feeling my devotion to you will enlarge my soul, and perhaps a few other things as well — but for all that you are, I will remain your true and faithful friend. Stacy

Ode to Chocolate

chocolate

WHY | I can't imagine that you really need an explanation for this. I'm a woman, and I do much better with at least a smidgen of chocolate every single day.

WHERE | In the *All About Us* album, behind the *Stacy* tab.

WHAT | If you think a photo shoot with your kids is fun, just wait until you set up something with your favorite chocolate treats. I laid one piece of brown cardstock down on my kitchen counter and leaned another up to cover the back-splash. This, plus the natural light streaming in my window, made me think I could have a second career as a food stylist. Hmmm... Seriously though, start taking pictures of the "things" you love.

Are the pictures you take helping you tell a complete story of your life? If you're like me, you may decide to take fewer photos at birthday parties and more photos of the little things that define you, like chocolate!

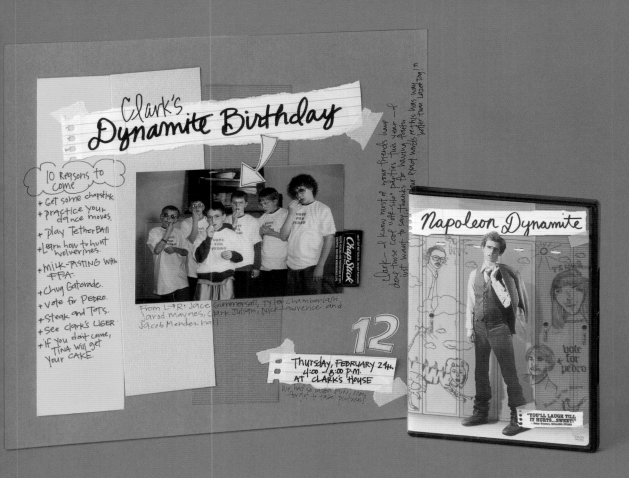

Clark's
Dynamite Birthday

10 reasons to come
+ Get some chapstick
+ practice your dance moves.
+ play TetherBall
+ Learn how to hunt wolverines.
+ Milk-tasting with FFA.
+ Chug Gatorade.
+ vote for Pedro.
+ Steak and Tots.
+ See Clark's LIGER
+ if you don't come, Tina will get your CAKE.

From L→R: Jace Gummersall, Tylor Chamberlain, Jarod Maynes, Clark Julian, Nick Lawrence, and Jacob Mendenhall.

Clark—I know most of your friends have done these cool 'off-site' parties this year—I just want to say thanks for having fun with your card words graphics has won better than Laser Tag.

12

Thursday, February 24th
4:00 – 8:00 P.M.
at Clark's House

We had so much fun, Mom forgot to take pictures!

Napoleon Dynamite

vote for pedro

"YOU'LL LAUGH TILL IT HURTS...SWEET!"

clark's dynamite birthday

WHY | Birthdays are milestones and I love creating birthday party pages almost as much as I love planning unforgettable birthday parties! Since the movie *Napoleon Dynamite* was such a big hit this year, it was the obvious choice for Clark's party theme.

WHERE | In the *Family Celebrations* album, behind the *Birthdays* tab.

P.S. When this section grows too large, I plan to pull the birthday pages out and put them in their own album called Family Birthdays. Remember: Scrapbooking is not a science. It's a dynamic, changing collection of your life's stories. You don't have to know where everything will ultimately end up—you can always move things around later. Don't forget this, okay?

WHAT | I was very excited about the details of this party, and I had a photo checklist a mile long. Guess what? I took the group shot after everyone arrived, put my camera on the piano and never picked it up again (whoops.) I learned that it was okay. I actually had more fun as mom-immersed-in-party vs. mom-with-camera madly shooting pictures. I haven't asked, but I bet Clark had more fun too! He said, as I tucked him in bed, "This was way better than going to Laser Tag. Thanks, Mom."

I am their demographic

WHY | Target is just plain one of my favorite places to go. The fact that I can get stuff I need there is a huge bonus. Call it the democratization of good design or affordable style—it speaks to my head, my handbag and my heart. That's a winning combination.

WHERE | In the *Places We Go* album, behind the *Close to Home* tab.

WHAT | The Coluzzle circle-cutter is a tool I'm gratefully rediscovering, thanks to a recommendation from Donna Downey, friend and contributing editor at the magazine.

Just Mom and Chase 8/04

places tag

The sky's the limit here. I think you should record both the places you most want to see before you die and the places you see on a routine basis. From the supermarket and library to your dream destinations, places are a part of us. This tag will encourage you to make them a part of your scrapbook.

Boston

WHY | To remember the weekend trip Chase and I took to Boston. I taught at a scrapbook convention and we spent a day and half sight-seeing.

WHERE | In the *Places We Go* album, behind the *Far Away* tab.

WHAT | Sometimes your photos work better if you turn your paper sideways (unless you're working on a 12 x 12 layout—in this case you're stuck.) What I really learned is that something magical happens when a mom spends time alone with just one child. I wouldn't trade a million bucks—and I'm totally serious—for the time I spent with Chase in Boston.

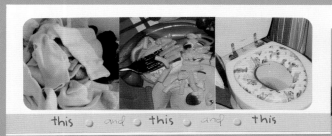

this ● and ● this ● and ● this

79 unmatched socks!

and this ●

Someday in the not too distant future I will come home and the house will be quiet. The pillows will be on the chairs and the only socks to pick up will be Daddy's socks. Someday I won't have to flush the toilet every time I walk by the bathroom. Someday I won't buy Mac-n-cheese by the case at Costco. It's hard to believe now, but someday I will miss these very ordinary and often frustrating sights, and I'm making this page to remind me of that.

● Someday you'll be gone and I'll miss all this.

Now... please, please go pick up the socks!!

all this

this and this and this

WHY | I've learned to see my everyday routine, frustrations and all, with a fresh perspective—one that makes me more appreciative, kind, patient and satisfied. And it's all because of my passion for scrapbooking. Cool hobby.

WHERE | In the *Things We Do* album, behind the *Everyday Life* tab.

WHAT | I'm comfortable with the disarray that I live in and the imperfect way in which I'm documenting it—my life is just right for me. I hope you'll set aside one day to photograph the stuff that seems mundane. These pictures, more than most that you've taken, will become the evidence of a purposeful, productive life. It's *this*— at least as often as the vacations and parties— that you will reminisce about.

May 2005
Joy School
Tavin · Caleb · Cody · Taft
Perhaps you're familiar with the story - a weary traveler, a poor village and a magic stone — the magic of course is how the villagers each add but one 'ingredient' and a savory soup is made.
Making Stone Soup is one example of the fun and clever activities Taft and I enjoyed this year as mothers came together to teach a curriculum full of Joy.
Delicious Memories!
Stone
Soup.

stone soup

WHY | Taft and I were part of a cooperative preschool this year. I need at least one page to remind us! On this particular day, we sat on the kitchen floor around a big metal stock pot. I read the story "Stone Soup," while the boys added the ingredients to our own group effort.

WHERE | Our *School of Life* albums start with kindergarten, but that doesn't mean I can't put a layout or two about preschool in the front!

WHAT | One scrapbook page can represent an entire year in school. I've taken other preschool related photos this year, but this page is really all I need. I've got the four little boys who were a part of our school and a description of one very happy memory. I can do additional pages later, but I think I'll call it good for now.

Sometimes I use my computer to compose what I want to say before I write it on my page, but most of the time I just do a quick practice-write in pencil and then go over it in pen. A white eraser easily removes the pencil lines.

scooter

W H Y | I got a green scooter for my 40th birthday! I've waited a long time, and it's a long story, so I plan to type up all the details and place it behind the layout in the page protector.

W H E R E | In the *All About Us* album, behind the *Stacy* tab.

W H A T | Less really is more. I had several detail photos of my scooter and several different accents that I thought would work on the page, but I discovered that it was just too much. I took the good advice of my friend, MaryRuth, and removed accents that didn't "feel" right. Having someone you can "run things by" is just one advantage of scrapping with friends.

Oregon coast

W H Y | Because we took a weekend trip to the ocean and I've been waiting for a reason to scrapbook it. This book is helping me get so many pages done!

W H E R E | In the *Places We Go* album, behind the *Far Away* tab.

W H A T | I actually like waiting to scrapbook some events. I've had these photos for almost two years. Pulling them out now, I'm able to easily select the ones I really want to use, because my short-term memory has given way to general impressions and an overall fondness for the setting, which helps me create a strong mood with the design. Don't stress about letting pictures sit—it's okay, and maybe even good.

Ya gotta love the square punch. Is there a handier tool for getting lots of photos on the page, or getting the most out of each photo? I love punching two small "details" from one 4 x 6 photo!

Whenever I say to my boys "Guess where we get to go?" Someone invariably shouts out is it **THE LAMBSONS**? Since we live in Washington and they live in Utah—the answer is usually no, but I love that spending time with them is so high on my kids' list. The Lambson's home has been our home for 2 weeks each summer—since I've worked for the magazine, and honestly, there isn't another group of people anywhere that are cooler, kinder or more FUN than Don, Deanna, Nick, Benji, Peter, Levi, Noah and Maya!

JUN 2003
JUL 2003
OCT 2003

the Lambsons

W H Y | Because if I could "extend" my extended family to include anyone, it would be these guys. Don and Deanna and their five boys (and new baby girl) are the coolest, most generous and most wonderful people I know.

W H E R E | In the *People We Love,* behind the *Friends* tab.

W H A T | I like scrapbooking people. Not because of what they are doing or where they are going, but because of who they are. Who are your family's closest friends? Do you have a page that pays tribute to who they are and what they mean to you?

And, put down the ruler and paper trimmer and pick up a pair of scissors from time to time. Things don't always have to be so straight! Did you notice how I just cover up my mistakes? That's okay, too.

The scrapbook layout contains the following handwritten and typographic text:

LORI

HOT BATHS 25¢ Soap &...

EVERY NOOK AND CRANNY

HOME

LORI – your space defines you my friend. Everything tells a story – speaks to your love of the past and the secrets it holds. This is what your children will remember (yes, the bathroom.) Let me know when you're ready to scrapbook with me.

Forget the piles of photos my love and tell your story.

where'd ya get the cool blue glass any way?

LIGHT

Use the tags to tell me more (please) you installed the sink yourself?

Beautiful antiques

TREASURES

every nook and cranny

W H Y | I'm trying to get my dear friend Lori into scrapbooking, but her piles are paralyzing. Sound familiar? I don't know another person as resourceful as Lori. She just installed a new sink in an antique cabinet for her basement bathroom. She's so creative, and I know if she could just let go of that "all or none" mentality she could create some really meaningful albums. If you're like Lori, please know:

1. You don't have to organize your photos before you begin. In fact, this is likely to discourage, not encourage!

2. You should continue to take lots of photos and focus on everyday stuff, like your recent home improvement project!

3. What your children want most from you is your story. Make a page a month. Start with a memory. Add a few photos. Don't make it hard.

W H E R E | I'm giving this page to Lori in an 8½ x 11 album (with a bunch of empty page protectors).

W H A T | I'm going to make permanent space in my studio for my sewing machine; I like the look of real stitching!

friends tag

The dictionary says a friend is someone attached to you by feelings of affection or personal regard. This tag is probably not roomy enough for a comprehensive list of people who fit this description, but start the list anyway. I bet you'll be surprised at the pictures you need to take and the pages you want to create.

Down deep in every human soul is
a hidden longing, impulse, and ambition
to do something fine and enduring.

GRENVILLE KLEISER

projects

mom according to...

WHY | Angie Lucas, managing editor at the magazine, gave me the assignment to learn more about myself by interviewing one of my children. The plan was to share the resulting page in an article, but I so enjoyed the off-the-cuff responses I got from one boy that I decided to interview all four and compile the results in a fun office-inspired album from SEI. Angie agreed to let me share *Mom, According to Clark, Chase, Trey and Taft* in this book!

I asked each of my boys the same 20 questions (see page 66), and transferred their "unedited" responses to a two-page spread featuring their photo. My friend Amy, a photographer, took a special black-and-white group shot for my title page.

WHERE | Right now, it's in the top drawer of my nightstand. I think I'll pull it out each year on Mother's Day. I also think I'll interview the boys about their dad next year.

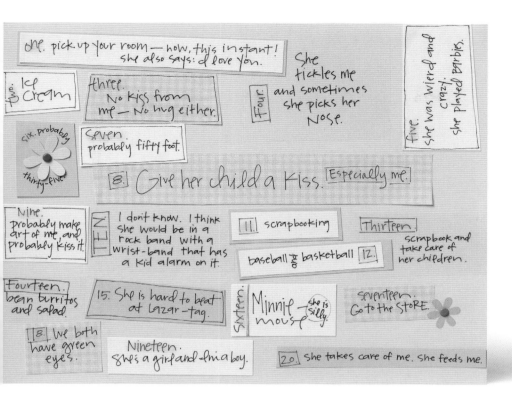

One. pick up your room — now, this instant! she also says: I love you.

We Ice Cream

three. No Kiss from me — No hug either.

Four She tickles me and sometimes she picks her nose.

five. She was wierd and crazy. she played Barbies.

six. probably thirty-five!

Seven. probably fifty foot.

8 Give her child a kiss. Especially me.

Nine. Probably make art of me, and probably kiss it.

TEN I don't know. I think she would be in a rock band with a wrist-band that has a kid alarm on it.

11 scrapbooking

Thirteen scrapbook and take care of her children.

baseball & basketball 12

Fourteen. bean burritos and salad.

15. She is hard to beat at Lazar-tag.

Sixteen. Minnie mouse she is silly

seventeen. Go to the STORE.

18 We both have green eyes.

Nineteen. She's a girl and I'm a boy.

20 She takes care of me. She feeds me.

TITLE PAGE

Mom according to trey

WHAT | My boys are growing up. Clark's answers were amazingly accurate. I didn't realize he knew so much about my likes and dislikes. Trey reported that my favorite thing to do is to, "Give her child a kiss—especially me." He's right. When asked what I do when he is not around, he responded, "Probably make art of me and kiss it."

Self-esteem is healthy! Seriously though, moms often feel that much of what they do goes unnoticed. Each one of my boys mentioned specific ways they feel my love—and all I had to do was ask!

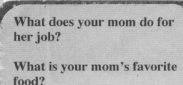

What does your mom do for her job?

What is your mom's favorite food?

What makes you proud of your mom?

If your mom were a cartoon character, who would she be?

think about it

You could create an interview album like this for anyone—a friend, sibling or teacher. You could even interview a group of people about an event like a family reunion or a time period—say the 2005 soccer season.

I put four interview questions on the back of each monogram coaster. The coasters spell my name and are tucked in the page protector with the title page.

interview questions

1. What is something mom always says to you?
2. What makes mom happy?
3. What makes mom sad?
4. How does mom make you laugh?
5. What was mom like as a child?
6. How old is your mom?
7. How tall is your mom?
8. What is her favorite thing to do?
9. What does your mom do when you're not around?
10. If your mom becomes famous, what will it be for?
11. What is your mom really good at?
12. What is your mom not very good at?
13. What does your mom do for her job?
14. What is your mom's favorite food?
15. What makes you proud of your mom?
16. If your mom were a cartoon character, who would she
17. What do you and your mom do together?
18. How are you and your mom the same?
19. How are you and your mom different?
20. How do you know your mom loves you?

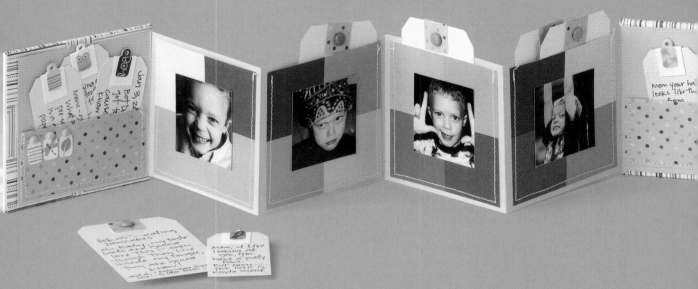

trey

WHY | My friend Allison was in town, helping me prepare for an upcoming scrapbooking event, and we took a break one afternoon to make little accordion pocket books. I have wanted to gather some of Trey's most memorable quotes for awhile, and as I was stitching pockets, I suddenly knew this would be the perfect place. I would combine photos and words to create a tribute called simply *Trey*.

WHERE | I envision someday having a cool basket, bowl or tray in my family room to display a bunch of these snack-sized scrapbooks. They will be chock full of personality and make great conversation starters!

WHAT | Two things. One, I'm loving the little 2-inch square photos from *scrapbookpictures.com*. I simply went into my digital photo files, found four personality shots of Trey, and ordered them in 2-inch black-and-white. Two, my family file really works! I keep several little "writer's notebooks" around my house, so I can jot down, among other things, quirky things my kids say. I periodically rip the pages out of these notebooks and file the loose pieces of paper behind each person's tab. My file enabled me to quickly find dozens of quotes to tuck into the pockets of Trey's book.

defining moments tag

Some moments define or redefin
you—getting an education,
marriage, giving birth. Others
sneak by without much fanfare,
but they leave an indelible mark
of redirection on your life. This
tag is for your defining moments
with the hope that they make it
into your scrapbook story. How
have you been challenged and
changed by opportunities seized

close to my heart

WHY | When I was invited to speak at a Close to My Heart convention in 2004, I decided to make a page to honor its founder, Jeanette Lynton, whom I've known since my days as a D.O.T.S. demonstrator. (D.O.T.S. eventually became Close To My Heart.) When I sat down to look through my photos, I got caught up in a whole bunch of memories and was reminded of what a pivotal period this was in my life—the beginning of an unplanned career in scrapbooking. I listed my top ten memories as a D.O.T.S. demonstrator and decided an envelope mini-album would be the perfect place to pair my recollections and random photos.

WHERE | It belongs in my studio as a reminder to me of the serendipity of it all—and so it sits on a shelf with some of my rubber stamps. I made two sets of journaling tags: one resides in my mini-album and I placed the other one on a jump ring and gave it to Jeanette during my presentation (that felt really good).

WHAT | When you start out to make a page and find you have more memories and emotion than you initially realized, a mini-album might be the answer. Remember, the size, shape, and ultimate resting place of a scrapbooked memory is less important than the fact that you did what felt right.

7 Background and Texture Paper!

What can I say? I am a stampaholic with a serious addiction to rubber. Stamps are so versatile and easy to use. Even though I don't get to play with my stamps as much as I'd like now I love to display them on my walls in my studio. I have two walls in IKEA cabinets—36 drawers in all full of stamps—OK and two boxes in my crawl space too. I love each and every one but my all-time favorites are Frank and Easter Daisies. Scarlett, This Much Bear, love my super sizes I love my Words To Live By set (which I like to think Jenette created just alphabets and my for me) I LOVE STAMPS!

think about it

You can easily celebrate a time period in your past in the engaging format of an envelope album. List your top ten memories from high school, a summer job, your post-college graduation road trip, etc... Each item on your list gets one envelope/pocket in the album, so there's plenty of room for photos, journaling and meaningful memorabilia. You could even scrapbook ahead of time some series of events you're looking forward to, like I did here as a Christmas gift for my husband, to anticipate our 2005 date nights. When he returned the TiVo I gave him last year, he basically sent me the message that he wants scrapbook gifts for the rest of his life—full of love and completely nonrefundable—ha!

where in Spokane

WHY | It's hard to believe, but after ten years of moving every other year or so, we've been settled in Spokane, Washington for five whole years. This celebrates our Spokane home and a few of the surrounding places that we've grown to love.

WHERE | In our guest bedroom, on top of the big picture book of Spokane history.

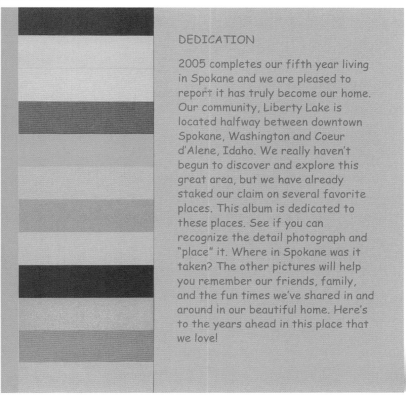

DEDICATION

2005 completes our fifth year living in Spokane and we are pleased to report it has truly become our home. Our community, Liberty Lake is located halfway between downtown Spokane, Washington and Coeur d'Alene, Idaho. We really haven't begun to discover and explore this great area, but we have already staked our claim on several favorite places. This album is dedicated to these places. See if you can recognize the detail photograph and "place" it. Where in Spokane was it taken? The other pictures will help you remember our friends, family, and the fun times we've shared in and around in our beautiful home. Here's to the years ahead in this place that we love!

WHAT | Scrapbooking the places that have meaning to you is a very rewarding thing to do. I love approaching memories from different perspectives, and I'm continually amazed at the importance of beloved places—from the historic district of a city to something as familiar as the ice-cream shop you patronize several times a year to celebrate special events. Places are the stage where our memories are played out—the backdrop that we generally don't miss until it's gone. The cool thing is you probably don't need additional photos to scrapbook this way; you just need to look at the photos you have differently.

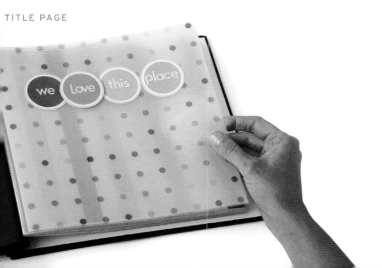

SECTION OPENER

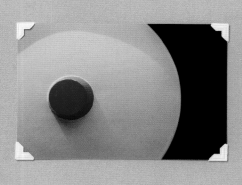

FILLER PAGES

RIVERFRONT PARK is located downtown Spokane and covers more than 100 acres. It features tree-lined paths, spacious lawns, park benches, a variety of public art and sculpture and various venues including the Spokane Opera House and an IMAX Theater.

The park had its origins as the site for Expo '74, the World's Fair, and subsequently was preserved as a landmark park popular with local citizens as well as out-of-town visitors. At the center of the park is the Spokane River and falls. In addition to an amusement area that doubles as an ice rink in the winter, Riverfront Park also boasts a 1909 Looff Carousel, a giant Radio Flyer wagon and slide, a garbage-eating goat, the clock tower that stood in the midst of the original train station and a gondola ride across the river.

Our family loves Riverfront Park. We almost always purchase summer passes and love taking along friends and visitors. We see IMAX movies, go on rides, eat picnics, feed ducks and seagulls, rent bikes and surreys --- walk, talk and relax.

WE LOVE THIS PLACE!

think about it

You could list five to ten places around your home (parks and recreational areas, day-trip destinations, restaurants, schools—even the mall!) and set up a file for each. Now, spend 30 minutes looking through photos. I bet you'll find several taken in these various locations. As you browse your pictures, you'll probably discover other places to add to your list. As you continue taking pictures at various events, get in the habit of filing a few in these "places" files. This is what I call "photo triage" and it is simply the process by which you decide how a photo might best be used in your scrapbooks. Photo triage will open you up to all kinds of cool connections and meaningful projects. Learn all the details of photo triage in the special issue *Easy Organization*, available at *simplescrapbooksmag.com*.

Individual photos don't need a name and date. Keep your design clean by devoting one page to journaling and letting yourself enjoy just pictures on the other pages.

SECTION OPENER   FILLER PAGES

Head straight north on Argonne and you'll end up
in GREENBLUFF, a community of family farms
and orchards, well known to residents of
Spokane. From early summer until late fall, you'll
find home baked pies and ice-cream, country
gifts, antiques, farm animals and lots of
downhome friendly folk, and it's all just 45
minutes away!

We love to drive to Gleenbluff to pick apples
and pumpkins in the fall. It's fun to look back at
our pictures and see how the boys grow from
year to year. We always look forward to
escaping the city for breathtaking views, corn
mazes, fun farm activities and fresh fruit right
off the trees! If you come to visit the Julians
when the weather's warm, we promise to take
you to Greenbluff for the day!

WE LOVE THIS PLACE!

try it!

To create an album like this, you'll need the
following framework pages:

Title page
The name and location of your album goes here.

Dedication page
Why do you want to create this album, why now?
Explain here why you're creating the album—
what does the place mean to you?

Closing page
You might want to include a map on the closing
page of your album, or just a big photo of your
family in front of your home or the "Welcome to
Your City" sign.

Sections
You will also need a five-page section for each
"place" you want to tribute:

Opener—Place one 4 x 6 detail shot here. You
probably don't have a picture like this yet, so plan
to take one on your next visit.

Pages one and two—Arrange eight to ten snapshots taken in this place on these pages, and use
photos from different times. This makes the visual
collage more interesting. Now, think of one word
that best describes what you do or how you feel in
this place. Use that word as an accent on page two.

Page three—This page is for journaling. Start
with some historical information or a general
description, and then share your specific memories
and feelings. Why do you love this place?

Page four—A few final photos go here, and perhaps
a piece of memorabilia if you have it.

materials file

Once I have a concept for a theme album, I begin gathering the photos and products that I will use to create it. I keep all of these materials in a Materials File. This simple storage solution is one of the best time savers I know. Time is a precious commodity, and when I eek a little out of my crazy life to finish or update an album, all I have to do is grab the materials file for that project and get to work.

I use and really like the Croppin' Companion for my materials files. They are exceptionally sturdy, have several pockets, and they look so cute tagged and stacked side by side in my studio. For more information visit **croppincompanion.com**.

Simplify the design process by planning your album and keeping materials together until you have finished it.

family 2005

W H Y | Since Junkitz introduced their adorable line of clothing labels, I have wanted to design an album around them. Hats off to the dozens of dedicated manufacturers who make hundreds of inspiring products!

W H E R E | Sitting on a tiered "memory" shelf in my living room. My grandfather's antique typewriter sits on the big bottom shelf. There's also a miniature trunk full of letters written by family members and myself during my first year in college. And now, amidst a variety of vacation trinkets, sits my *Family 2005* album. I might move it to another place someday, but for now it has a home.

W H A T | Add just a few words to the right picture and you really can "freeze" in time a loved one's personality. I simply used the seven words (*Is, Has, Can, Watches, Reads, Wishes* and *Needs*) to prompt descriptive words and phrases for each member of my family. Add a title page and a photo of your current home and you've got a family treasure that screams "Pick me up!" to display in your home. Trust me, after a few mini-albums like this, the piles of "unscrapped" pictures don't seem to matter any more.

DEDICATION PAGE

IS: 39
HAS: BROWN EYES, 20/400 VISION, 15"
BICEPS AND A BYU-BLUE HONDA CRV
CAN: PLAY THE PIANO BY EAR AND REMAIN
CALM AMIDST CHAOS
WATCHES: 24, AMERICAN IDOL, SURVIVOR
AND ULTIMATE MAKEOVER—HOME EDITION
READS: THE WALL STREET JOURNAL AND
HOW-TO-SPEAK-KOREAN BOOKS
WISHES: HE HAD MORE TIME TO GOLF AND
DO YOGA
NEEDS: LONG HOT SHOWERS AND LOVE

IS: 4
HAS: BROWN EYES, CURLY HAIR AND AN
UNTESTED BUT OBVIOUSLY HIGH IQ.
CAN: PLAY COMPUTER GAMES, BUILD GIANT
PUZZLES, AND RUN REALLY FAST. CAN ALSO
SPOT AND CALL OUT ALL "HONEYBUCKETS"
WHEN RIDING IN THE CAR.
WATCHES: THE SAME MOVIE SEVERAL TIMES IN
A ROW.
READS: SOON, VERY SOON — CURRENTLY
MASTERING HIS ABCS AND HIS NUMBERS!
WISHES: YOGURT DIDN'T HAVE LUMPS, AND
LITTLE BOYS DIDN'T HAVE TO WEAR SHOES
NEEDS: HIS FOUR SPECIAL BLANKIES AT TUCK-
IN, COLD CEREAL AND LOTS OF LOVE.

ten
things I love about my grandma

grandma addie

W H Y | I had to compile this scrapbook card for a product promotion in the *Simple Scrapbooks* booth at a CHA trade show. Of course, I waited until the night before I left to start, so I had to finish on the airplane. Picture this: me, in seat 22C, all emotional as I reflected on the relationship I have with my Grandma Addie. The flight attendant thought the card was really cool. I gave her the magazine website so she could order one for herself.

W H E R E | I gave this to my grandmother for her 94th birthday in June, along with some pretty pink flowers.

W H A T | It felt so good to express my love for my grandmother in this way. I know she appreciated my gift, but the most significant outcome wasn't the album I made, it was the opportunity it created for me to realize and write down my feelings.

Grandma Addie is not to going to be around much longer, but because I scrapbook, I recognize what she means to me now, while she is still here. I visited grandma over the 4th of July, and I asked about her dining room table and her piano and the picture called "Lady at the Opera" that hangs above her love seat. She talked and I listened. I noticed the way she moves her hands and I marveled at her ability to remember names and recall details as she told her stories. I chose to spend time with her, and I'm not sure I would have if I hadn't created this scrapbook card for her. Scrapbooking changes your perspective, and encourages you to slow down and take more delight in people and experiences. That's powerful stuff.

family tag

Most of your pictures probably include family, but are you really sharing what makes each person unique and valued? Make a list of immediate family members here. Every time you scrapbook an aspect of their personality, put a tally mark next to their name. List also members of your extended family, so that you'll be reminded to take photos of them and write about how they influence your life. Perhaps it's time to scrapbook Uncle Bob or cousin Allen. What have you learned from them? Why do you look forward to seeing them?

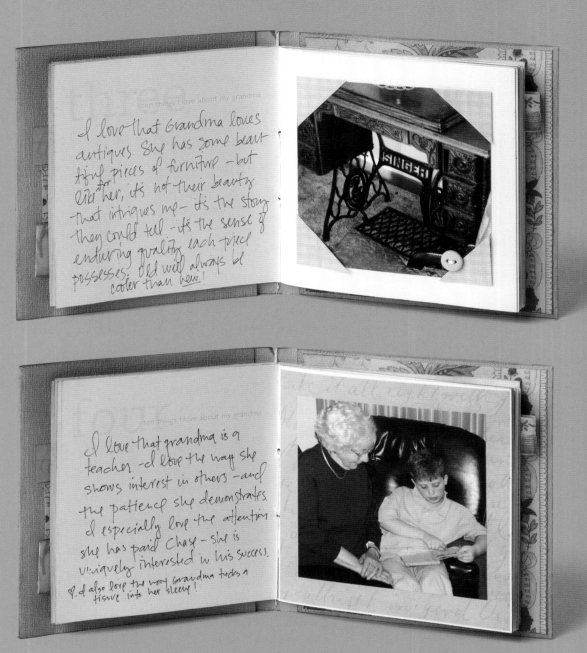

try it!

Little albums like these are so easy to create, you could make two for each member of your family—one to give away and one to keep one for yourself. By the end of a year, you will have a cool collection of colorful memories celebrating the people you love most.

think about it

This is "memory first" scrapbooking at it's best. I've led thousands of scrapbookers through my "two-minute memories" exercise over the years, but it wasn't until last February that I truly understood the power in simply closing your eyes and focusing all of your senses on one person. Immerse yourself like this for just one minute and specific, detailed memories surface. Spend another minute writing these random thoughts, recollections and emotions down and you have the content for a very meaningful tribute—with or without photos. Two minutes and one afternoon—now, that's doable!

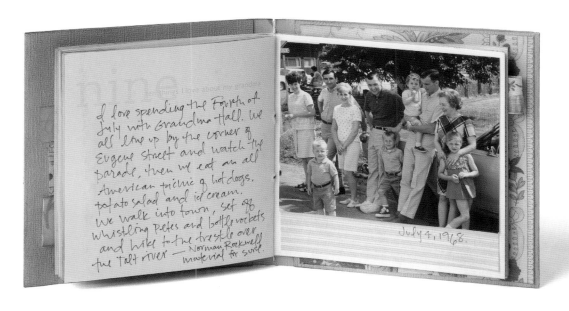

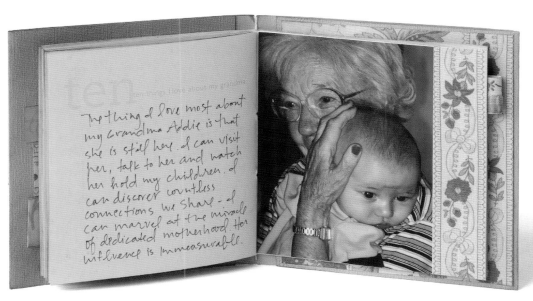

Two years later...
a book just for you ♥

May you remember and relive the magic again and again!

♥Mom

remember the magic

WHY | My youngest son Taft climbed up on the counter a month or so ago and asked when we were going back to DisneyWorld. He was just two when we vacationed there. Curious, I asked him what he liked best about DisneyWorld. He said, "Meeting Buzz Lightyear." I was amazed at this because he spent most of his time asleep in the stroller, and he's not even in the picture with Buzz.

I was also surprised by the list of other highlights Taft shared with me. I decided that morning I would revisit my two-year old Disney photos and create a little picture book just for him.

WHERE | We'll keep this album in Taft's room, on the dresser with his Mickey Mouse ears.

WHAT | My memories are not my children's memories. I'm so glad I didn't feel pressure to scrapbook all of my DisneyWorld photos after our trip, because I was able to go back and create this album just for Taft, with his memories in mind. I also discovered a fun use of Creative Memories albums. You can cut a shape out of the heavy strap-hinge pages and create little windows—a fun and interactive element for a young child.

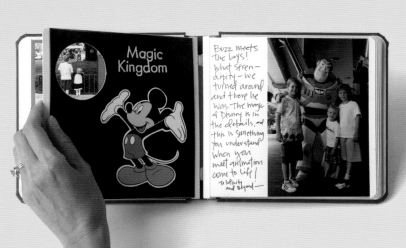

the food we will remember

W H Y | I've wanted to create a recipe album for a long time. I've actually started a couple of times and then abandoned the project. When I started again, I asked my boys, "What does Mom fix for you that's your favorite?" The list was short and quite revealing: Cold cereal, macaroni and cheese, waffles, banana bars, and yogurt with sprinkles. I knew cooking wasn't my forte, but I didn't realize just how obvious the evidence is. It isn't a recipe album that I need to create, but I a tribute to the food my kids will remember!

W H E R E | I think I'll display this one in my kitchen—maybe in the corner, by the cookie jar. (I do bake cookies.) I'll stand it up on a small easel, a suggestion from Donna Downey.

W H A T | This album was so much fun to create. I did it in one day, and I kept running upstairs to cut up labels and box tops. I even sent my babysitter to the store for those little stickers they put on bananas and tomatoes. Luckily, I have a photo file for "kids and food" where I've been sticking pictures for 10-plus years. I put my pile of pictures in front of me, along with my food ephemera and 4 x 4 squares of cardstock. From there, I just started slapping pages together with no particular order in mind. I did slip the four or five "recipes" that I can truly claim in pockets at the back of the album.

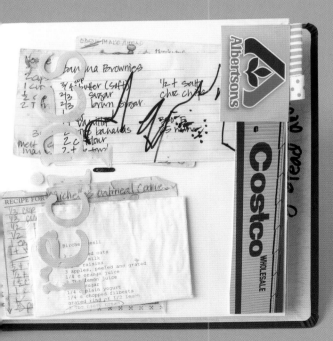

food tag

The senses of smell and taste are the strongest memory triggers, and both are strongly associated with food. So many memories are tied up in food, and is there anything better? What foods remind you of childhood? What foods do you serve in each season, or for specific holidays? Which specific food do you associate most with each of your closest friends? Food is festive, fabulous and totally fun to photograph. Start a list of favorites here and see what happens next!

26.2

WHY | Because I've always wanted to run a marathon, and I finally did it!

WHERE | I don't know yet—maybe in my studio.

WHAT | Besides the fact that long-distance runners regularly lose toenails, what I learned from running is that the best way to celebrate a goal accomplished is to scrapbook it. Doing so is an opportunity to preserve a visual record of the preparation and the process, and a chance to reflect and record what you learned. In many ways, life is a marathon. I certainly found parallels that gave me insight into living. Crossing the finish line was amazing, but only because of my commitment to hang in there. I worried about being too slow, but my time was of zero importance when I ran down that chute. The best memory I have now, a year later, is the experience of running with my sister Darci, and the look on my husband's face when I got my second wind at mile 18.5. I say it's all about family and supporting one another.

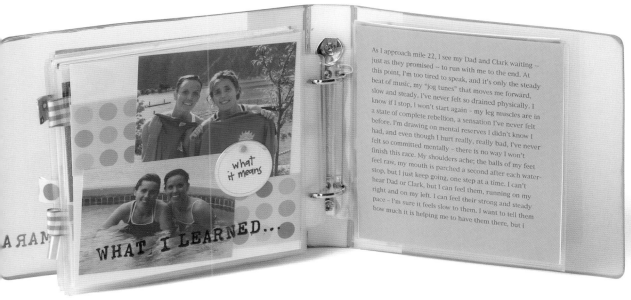

WHAT I LEARNED...

what it means

As I approach mile 22, I see my Dad and Clark waiting – just as they promised – to run with me to the end. At this point, I'm too tired to speak, and it's only the steady beat of music, my "jog tunes" that moves me forward, slow and steady. I've never felt so drained physically, I know if I stop, I won't start again – my leg muscles are in a state of complete rebellion, a sensation I've never felt before. I'm drawing on mental reserves I didn't know I had, and even though I hurt really, really bad, I've never felt so committed mentally – there is no way I won't finish this race. My shoulders ache; the balls of my feet feel raw, my mouth is parched a second after each water-stop, but I just keep going, one step at a time. I can't hear Dad or Clark, but I can feel them, running on my right and on my left. I can feel their strong and steady pace – I'm sure it feels slow to them, I want to tell them how much it is helping me to have them there, but I

can't. I can only think it and I do. I think it over and over and over again, and suddenly I picture in my minds eye, the family that has gone before me on this earth, and the family that will come after me and I see them, much like my father and my son running along – aware of me, pulling for me, running with me. It's an amazing view that opens up and I know for sure, something that I've only felt before – we are never alone. The race we call life is a team effort – we run our leg of the race not just for ourselves, but also for many, many others. As I turn the corner and see the finish, my father and my son fall back, and I cross the line all by myself. I have never felt so proud, and I say over and over "I did it." Happy tears of exhaustion fill my eyes. I can't believe it's finally over and I can't believe I did it. I just ran a marathon – but I couldn't have done it alone. Thank goodness I didn't have to. *Thanks Sis! Thanks Family.*

OUR SUPPORT TEAM

accomplishments tag

It might be athletic, academic or something much different altogether—
if it is something you worked hard to achieve, write it here. Perhaps
someone noticed and perhaps not. Either way, it's extraordinary that
you set out to do something and didn't give up. If you don't have photos,
don't worry. Just write about how you felt and include a piece of
memorabilia to remind you of the moment. Jot down, too, the goals you're
working on now so you won't forget to document them along the way!

postcard highlights

WHY | I found these funky postcards at the Denver airport on a layover and knew instantly that I could pair them with photos and make a clever and colorful collection of memories. I purchased three and then went online when I got home to buy the rest and a whole lot more (page 117). Totally cool company!

WHERE | Hanging on one of my pegboard shelves in my studio—so colorful!

WHAT | I love projects that bring together one photo from a variety of moments and events. They share a perspective that is otherwise not obvious, and it's very, very enlightening. Whether you use postcards or not, try sometime to match a photo with several of your favorite quotes; I guarantee you'll realize a few things as you look at your photos in this way.

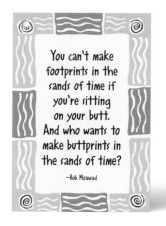

it's all about me

W H Y | Because I found this tin in the dollar section of my local Target and it made me wonder what I could put inside that really would be "All About Me." I challenged myself to gather and take photos of the things that might describe me if they were presented together to someone who knows me well.

W H E R E | With the other personality projects in the basket, bowl or tray that I will someday buy for our family room (see *Trey*, page 67).

W H A T | Women sometimes get caught up in roles and the expectations that go with them. This project requires no mention of any titles you bear or roles you play. It is simply a chance to celebrate you—the very essence of you. There are lots of people who love scented candles; fewer people who love scented candles, chunky bracelets and brownies, and no one but me who loves all of that *and* purchases micro-fine Uni-ball pens by the box, collects apple anything, should own stock in Chicos, and loves to run alone early in the morning.

The ordinary acts we practice everyday at home are of more importance to the soul than their simplicity might suggest.
~thomas Moore

think about it

Make your photo-journal even easier by scrap-booking each day for a week if a month seems overwhelming; or just take one photo a day and do less journaling. Another really cool way to use this idea would be to record the events of a month or week and then do it again in two, three or five years to compare and contrast the changes in your life. You can also make the project using just an inexpensive one-up photo album—the plastic kind you pick up at the photo counter. Or, you could make this a digital project. Burn one month of photos onto a CD with a voice report for each day. However you decide to do it, consider it the beginnings of your own encyclopedia of ordinary life (page 116).

may, everyday

WHY | I did a weekly journal of my youngest son, Taft's, first year, and since then I've been wanting to try a daily journal. I love the ease of scrapbooking in a photo album and this 6 x 12 album can be used with either full-page or 3-up protectors. I've combined both types to create space for two photos, one piece of memorabilia and lots of journaling each day for an entire month. The real reason behind my *May, Everyday* album is to record the details in my routine as a working mom surrounded by a chaotic household of young children. There is much about my "ordinary" life that's completely foreign to most people, and yet at the same time, some aspects of it probably feel familiar to many. I'm reading a book called *Encyclopedia of an Ordinary Life* (page 116) and it's fascinating and affirming. I wish it were easier for people to believe that their everyday stories are interesting. I really believe they are.

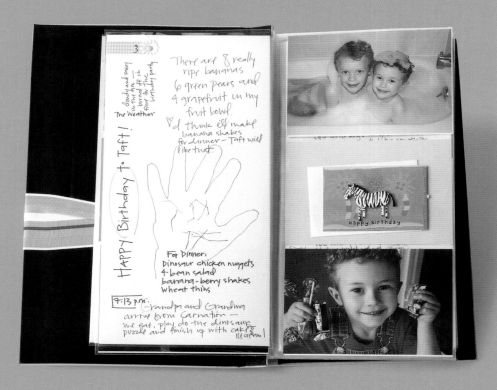

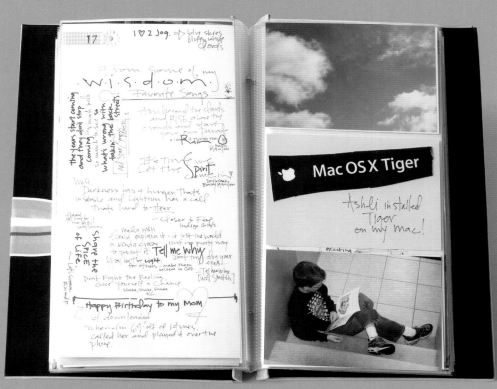

WHERE | Displayed, standing up like it is pictured here, on the bookshelves in our study.

WHAT | Gosh, I don't know where to begin. I learned so much doing this album. I learned to see photo opportunities all around me; I learned to watch for pieces of memorabilia that might be interesting; I learned that I really did have something different to say each day; I learned that I could record the not-so-rosy moments and not feel ashamed. I learned that things change fast—even in the course of a month; I learned to really appreciate one-hour digital developing. (I wanted to get my pictures back and inserted in my album quickly.) Finally, I learned that you can remove the spine insert from a post-bound album and tie ribbons to the posts—cute.

Since this project required a lot of writing, I assembled a portable handwriting tote (page 121). Sometimes I wrote early in the morning at the kitchen table, other times, I wrote late at night, tucked into bed.

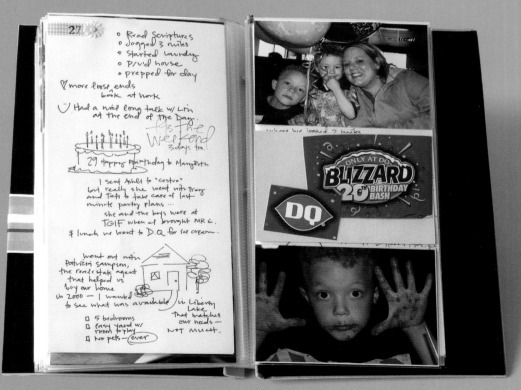

try it!

The easiest way to complete an album like this is to make the entire thing ahead of time. You'll need the following framework pages:

- A title page

- 2-page filler pages for each day of the month

- A closing page to summarize or record daily totals if you keep tallies like I did (see page at right).

Keep the design really clean by using repetitive elements (like my small daisy and brads) and select a color palette that speaks to the season of your album. Plan on using a couple of different cameras. You might want to purchase a disposable one to carry with you, to be sure you won't be without one when you need it.

Consider these titles, or make up one that suits you: *30 Days Hath September*; *December, One Day at a Time*; *A March Full of Memories*, or *It All Happened in June*. Based on my experience, I think you'll really enjoy this one.

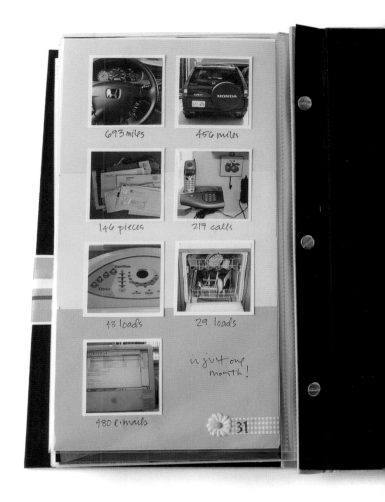

girl's weekend

WHY | My mom, two sisters, two sisters-in-law and my aunt gather once a year for a couple of days just to hang out together. This year, about a week before I left, I was wandering through Michaels and found these plain white canvas bags. The price was five for $4.99, so I stood there trying to think of a reason to buy them. The idea of a coordinating accordion album and little bag for each "girl" formed. I put the bags, buttons and flowers by my bed and sewed them on a few at a time before falling asleep each night. The little albums only took about 45 minutes to cut, fold and assemble.

WHERE | It's funny, one of my sisters asked me, "What am I supposed to do with this book in a bag?" and I replied "I dunno, but it sure was fun to make." I added, "I think I'm going to hang mine from a hook in my studio." Someone else suggested putting it in the same place you put special greeting cards you just can't throw away. Even if you don't look at it for years, it's sure to brighten your mood someday.

WHAT | On the last afternoon of our time together, we sat in a park and passed our mini-books around, taking turns writing notes to each other. While we're all very different, we are committed to spending time together, and I felt a unique appreciation for each person as I wrote to them. It was a chance to feel close to this part of my extended family and I am thankful for that.

I took "head shots" with the intention of placing them opposite our notes. I ordered six copies of each photo and sent them to everyone after our weekend was over.

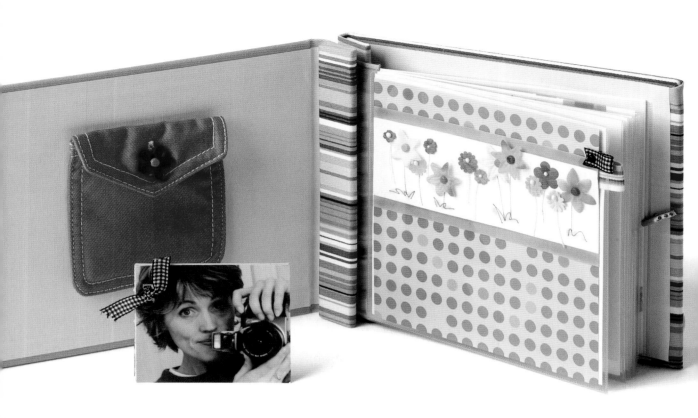

without a doubt

WHY | One word: Oprah! Even though I don't get to watch her show and I only read her magazine occasionally, I find her life and her commitment to empower and make a difference extremely inspiring. An idea for this album struck me over four years ago when reading her "What I Know for Sure" column. Subscribers to *"O" Magazine* received a collection of the thoughts she has shared in this column for the magazine's 5th anniversary. When I saw it, I thought, "Okay, it's time." I started jotting down ideas in various notebooks around my home and in my travel bag.

WHERE | I know this is going to sound crazy, but this one goes on a shelf in my laundry room, next to a passage from Nelson Mandela's inaugural address, which I found in Oprah's column. Some will think I'm a dork, but those that find value in

my big picture tag

This tag will become the "title page" for your tag book. Decorate it last, after you've spent time with all of the other tags. As you revisit the thoughts and insights recorded, you'll know what to write or display here.

positive affirmations will understand that I like to read the quote and the entries in this scrapbook while I fold clothes.

WHAT | Next to my *Photos I Love* album, this is my most treasured scrapbook and one that celebrates most meaningfully the things I know to be true.

I Have Lived

I am now old enough and experienced enough to realize that I can't begin to see, hear, feel, learn or understand the tiniest iota of what is available to me at this time in history.

I'd love to live abroad, scale the mountains of the world and have unlimited time to browse museums and libraries in exotic places. These opportunities may never present themselves, but still I can proclaim boldly that I have lived.

I've painted my toenails. I've touched the bark of a hundred-year-old tree. I've shopped online and eaten peas from my garden. I've made friends and probably a few enemies. I've stained my fingers picking blackberries, spilled perfectly good popcorn all over the theater floor, and wondered why clouds are white. I've given birth, given birthday presents and watched seagulls catch French fries mid-air. I've made promises and kept them. I've had canker sores, sunburns and a broken heart. I've jumped out of an airplane and slept in a tent.

I've saved a penny from the year I was born, and blue jeans that feel as though they were made for me. I've collected Lip Smackers and wristwatches and twice been in a live audience to hear The Mormon Tabernacle Choir sing "Battle Hymn of the Republic." I've read cereal boxes, written "wash me" across the back of a dusty car and skipped rocks on ponds and lakes. I've tucked children into bed and then returned to watch them sleep. I've smelled lilacs, gasoline and my grandmother's apple crisp pudding baking in my oven.

Yes, there is much to do and much more to see and try, but if I die tomorrow, please know that I have lived.

I Believe in God

I do, even amidst a general opinion that such a belief is hard to reconcile and often considered uneducated or ill-informed. I've decided that I would rather suffer a little social discomfort and err on the side of a religious perspective, than choose not to connect the intricacy of the human body, the beauty of nature, and the quiet whisperings of my soul to the existence of an all-wise, heavenly creator.

I believe in God. I believe that He is kind, that He injure in his name. I would never force these beliefs on another person, but at the same time I would be ashamed to discover something in my conduct that might discourage another's desire to believe.

I feel especially responsible to provide my children with an environment of acceptance while encouraging their spiritual world view, so they can confidently form personal knowledge that will be important in guiding their lives.

My belief in God has done nothing but strengthen me and bless my life, and it is without a doubt that I've

I've been thinking about...
scrapbooking

Do the kinds of things that come from the heart. When you do, you won't be dissatisfied, you won't be envious, you won't be longing for somebody else's things. On the contrary, you'll be overwhelmed with what comes back.

MORRIE SCHWARTZ

other stuff

chase ● trey ● stacy ● taft

geof ● clark

smile

Love you

If you only have one
Smile in
Give
the people
you

LOVE

Love you

FAMILY

FUN

big picture planning

To take advantage of your full potential, you need to step back occasionally from the creative process and consider your **motivation**, **approach** and **enjoyment**. Doing so will keep you on track and true to yourself. This is the thought process I followed to come up with my approach to scrapbooking (like my *Family Fun Library* and the other albums you'll read about in the following pages). Try my system, or use these checklists to invent one that works for you.

motivation

Why do you scrapbook? Sure, there are benefits and goals related to scrapbooking that appeal to scrapbookers everywhere. Ultimately, our personal motivations are unique and these motivations will change over time. They can, and should, change from page to page and album to album. You may not be scrapbooking now for the same reasons that motivated you to start—and that's okay. The important thing is to allow yourself to change. Think about the following objectives, and think about how much significance each has for you now.

Each time you begin a new project, pause to consider which objectives will guide your decisions. Is your goal to:

○ preserve and protect photographs?

○ record personal and family history?

○ enjoy a creative hobby?

○ spend time with friends or family members who also scrapbook?

○ express an interest/ability in photography and/or writing?

○ develop yourself personally with regard to design and/or artistic expression?

○ pursue opportunities in the scrapbooking/ papercrafting industry?

I hope as you conceive ideas for scrapbooks, you are taking advantage of the **Simple Scrapbooks Formula Worksheet**. This is a one-page guide designed to assist you in the planning and organization of any album. The Formula Worksheet can be found in each issue of **Simple Scrapbooks** magazine and online at **simplescrapbooksmag.com**.

approach

Check here the type of scrapbook albums you currently have; or the type of scrapbooks you would like to compile—or both! My list is, of course, not exhaustive; you are free to add to it if you like. Your approach—which is the format, organization and style of your scrapbooks—can be flexible. There is no reason you must scrapbook today in the same way you did five years, or even six months ago. This also means it is futile to try to set up a system/approach that will work for you, unchanged, two years from now. Don't worry about it.

Think about the primary motivation behind each album you checked. How did your objectives for these projects differ from one another? As you ponder the type of albums you could create, pause to establish your top two or three objectives for each. For example, one album might be a place to preserve and protect one-of-kind heritage photos in addition to stories from family members, while another is a coffee-table album intended to show-case select black-and-white photos from your trip to Europe. For some albums, it's perfectly acceptable to prioritize artistic expression first and personal history second, so you can use an album as a resume for a position on a design team. Knowing your objectives will ensure you spend your time and resources wisely.

○---- annual chronological scrapbooks for you and/or your immediate family

○---- albums for children to take with them when they leave home

○---- travel or vacation scrapbooks

○---- special event or milestone albums (birthday, graduation, wedding, anniversary, retirement)

○---- theme albums for special holidays, traditions, hobbies, etc.

○---- personal and/or historical tributes to people and places

○---- personal discovery books or photo journals

○---- showcase or photographic display albums and/or projects

○---- photo décor projects

○---- gift albums

enjoyment

Even with clear objectives and an exciting approach, it's also very helpful (and stress reducing) to think about (here I go again) the BIG picture. Ask yourself:

- Who is this scrapbook intended to please?

- How and by whom will this scrapbook be used?

  If you're creating an album to celebrate your child's budding personality and you imagine her looking at it as she falls asleep, a 12 x 12 album is probably not the "safest" presentation. An album that shares photos and insights from all 53 members of your extended family as a tribute to an 80-year-old grandfather may be unduly cumbersome in a small and very fat 6 x 6 album. Understanding that a particular album is not intended to thrill anyone outside your own home (i.e. win any contests) will alter how you approach it and make it more authentic and meaningful for the intended audience. It also allows you let go of a bunch of unnecessary creative pressure!

You might also consider asking:

- How and where will it be displayed? Will it:

  ○— sit on a shelf with other albums?

  ○— be given to someone as a gift?

  ○— be stored away, and brought out during a specific season or holiday?

  ○— be treated as part of the decor in a specific room in your home?

  ○— be portable, so it can travel with you or someone else?

Please remember that limiting yourself to just one objective, approach, size, album-type or storage plan will also limit your—and others—ability to enjoy your scrapbooking efforts. And that would be sad!

Okay...read that sentence again, because I'm serious. You aren't doing anyone a favor by holding out and refusing to be flexible!

For more information, instruction and free downloads on big-picture planning, visit my new website **bigpicturescrapbooking.com**.

stacy's albums: family fun library

You can probably tell by now that I don't scrapbook chronologically; I don't scrapbook pictures in the order they were taken or document events in the order they occur. Why? It's not fun for me, I don't recall memories in order, and I don't think presenting pages in sequential order is the most interesting way to share my stories. At some point, I also got tired of the guilt associated with feeling "behind" because I hadn't scrapbooked all my photos.

Instead, I have my *Family Fun Library*. It encourages me to focus less on how many photos I have and more on the people, places and things that are important to me. It also allows me to scrapbook my memories in any order I want. Not using a chronological system means that I don't have, say, a 2004 scrapbook. But it doesn't matter, because I have the key stories and memories from that year in my library.

To start a library of your own, buy an album for each of these categories:

All About Us is for your "personality" pages. It's where you celebrate what makes each member of your family unique and loved. Make a tab for each person in your immediate family and tabs, like *Oh Brother* for relationships between these people.

The People We Love album is for the other people in your life. I have sections for *Grandparents*, *Extended Family* and *Friends*.

The Places We Go is for everything from family vacations to local trips to your favorite hangouts. I have *Near and Far* tabs, plus a *Home* tab where I place pages about the homes we've lived in and other homes we love.

The coolest thing about this system is that I'm never "behind." In fact, I've stopped worrying about it entirely—and that has made scrapbooking so much more enjoyable!

The Things We Do album reflects your lifestyle. If your family participates in athletic events, you'll want a sports tab; if you're into gardening, a gardening tab. I have a tab for *Everyday Life*, *Accomplishments*, *Traditions*, and *Sports and Recreation*.

Using a library system like this helps you think differently about your memories. Since you don't store completed pages according to date, it's easier to sort photos into meaningful topics (like camping trips, Grandma's house, Dad and me) and create pages that bring together photos from different times. When you scrapbook an event, you get to choose what you want to emphasize: the personality of a family member, a place you love to go, or an activity that brings you joy. That's where you'll put the page!

If you have pictures of your son playing in the park with a friend, you could scrapbook the park where they are playing (*Places We Go*), the friendship (*People We Love*) or your son's silliness and curiosity (*All About Us*)—there is no wrong category!

I started my library in 2000, and it's still working for me. In fact, it's thriving! I love the flexibility. Some tabs have grown into volumes, but the fun and inviting structure stays the same. My children can easily find and revisit their favorite people, places and things!

stacy's albums: school of life

If you've got kids, you might feel some obligation to scrapbook for them. I understand. I bet you also know the overwhelming feeling that comes from realizing that your son, now eighteen, is only eight in his scrapbook! Don't panic. Yes, your son would love a scrapbook about his life. No, he doesn't need 15 volumes. Simplify! Let go of the guilt. Your children will appreciate a scrapbook of any size from you, and they may ultimately appreciate it being less than more.

I shared a concept I call *School of Life* in my book *Simple Scrapbooks* (2000). I'm sharing it again, because it's not only still working for me, it's the reason I'm able to work at the magazine, write articles, travel and teach, and still have time to explore fun scrapbooking topics and projects like those I've shared in this book. I love, love, love my *School of Life* albums. Better yet, my children love them.

Here's how it works: I scrapbook five pages for each year my boys are in school. That's it. That's all I need to do to stay current with their lives. Trey's kindergarten section of his *School of Life* is pictured at left. Page one and two contain school-related photos; a picture of the first and last day of school, the official school photo, and a sampling of other snapshots. Pages two and three showcase one picture from major life events of the year. This is where you'll find a birthday party photo, holiday photos, a personality shot or two, and a photo with friends and family members. Page five is a pocket page. Tucked inside are a few things that will have meaning in years to come: a selection of school papers, letters from grandparents, a few pieces of memorabilia, etc. Each year, I do essentially the same thing. The colors and style of my pages can change, but the time requirement does not!

Now, there are obviously hundreds of photos that never make it into my children's albums. That's okay! Because what I do include is all about them, and it's fun to look at and share with others. When my kids are grown, I'll send them off with two or three albums that hold the story of all their growing up years. Any additional pages I create about my children go in the **Family Fun Library**, which will stay with me.

stacy's albums

photos i love

I wish every scrapbooker would start a *Photos I Love* album. Over the years, I've created hundreds of pages and dozens of theme albums, but if I had to choose just one to keep, I'd choose this one. Why? Because it showcases my favorite photos from all times and places and my feelings about them. There is more sincere sentiment in this little album than any other single album I've made. The next time you're sorting photos and one catches you in an "Ohhh"—start a new pile, called *Photos I Love*. Set aside some time to write about it and I promise you'll treasure it forever.

family celebrations

This album is a place for me to collect pages about celebrations in my immediate and extended family. I have sections for *Births and Baby Blessings*, *Birthdays*, *Graduations*, *Weddings*, and *Family Parties and Reunions*. It is the album we pull off the shelf when family gathers to enjoy a milestone event. I'm currently putting birthday pages for my children in this album, but I may end up pulling them out and putting them in a separate birthday book.

just because

If you're like me, you sometimes end up with pages that don't seem to fit anywhere. My *Family Fun Library* is for 8½ x 11 pages but every now and then, for a class or a magazine assignment or just because I want to, I create 12 x 12 pages and don't really have a place to put them. I've had such a fun time writing this book and thinking about why I make pages and what I learn in the process, that I want to share that kind of information along with these "misfits" in a *Just Because* format. Who knows? It just might become a favorite!

Halloween

Hands down, this is my kids' favorite album. I bring it out during the month of October. It showcases one costume page per kid per year, plus a few party pages thrown in for fun. I created a fabric-covered album way back in 1994, which had to be replaced last year due to over-handling. I opted for a sturdy, black, 3-ring binder from the office supply store. Since I couldn't seem to part with the happy memories of the original cover, I simply pulled it off and slid it down inside the plastic window of the new binder.

Sing-along

I realized a while back that for me, scrapbooking isn't about the pictures. I want to focus on my memories and look at my pictures as an endless pile of illustrations. I have tons of memories associated with the songs I've sung over the years. This album holds fun pages that record, with colorful images, the words of these songs. You'll find preschool songs, folk songs, church hymns, anthems, and songs from our alma mater. I think I'm going to replace the album soon, just to give it an updated look.

Christmas exchange

Every year, my parents, my four siblings, and myself create a 2-page spread that features highlights of each of our families. The pages are organized by year, with a section page for each year. It's the only chronological album I have. We love referring to the book when we need to answer questions like "When did Uncle Kevin graduate?" or "What year was cousin Skye born?" Pulling this album out during the holidays gives us an opportunity to reflect on the challenges we've all faced and the blessings of extended family.

creativity

Above all, watch with glittering eyes
the whole world around you, because
the greatest secrets are always hidden
in the most unlikely places. Those who
don't believe in magic will never find it.

ROALD DAHL

Teaching scrapbook classes across the country has given me the opportunity to meet lots of women. Without exception, one of the most common concerns I hear, from New York to Newport Beach is, "I'm just not creative!" "But you are," I insist, "you just haven't learned how to recognize it." Why? Generally, people (including scrapbookers) associate creativity with a specific outcome, like inventing something new or winning a prize. But, creativity is not the means to an end—it's just the means. It can't be cajoled, coerced or controlled. It has to be nurtured and appreciated without any purpose beyond that of simply enjoying what it contributes to your life. I believe personal creativity is the practiced ability to experience the world in original ways: first, to notice something that others don't take the time to see; and second, to make it interesting or meaningful in a new context. By this definition, anyone can be creative.

Now, I realize this is sounding a bit esoteric. You're probably thinking, "Whatever, Stace. What's your point?" It's simply this: **Cultivate creativity and life will be more interesting.** You'll be surprised and delighted by your everyday world, and you'll see the novelty in things you've overlooked before. Creativity isn't what you do with paper, stickers or paint. It's how you think and make connections between all the incoming and the outgoing, and it is the single most important thing you can do to improve your big picture approach to scrapbooking. So keep reading.

With age, most of us lose the sense of wonder and the curiosity we had as children. Without this sense of wonder, life becomes routine. The best thing you can do to recognize your personal creativity is to simply **become more aware.** Practice a child-like curiosity and your view of the world will always remain fresh.

Next, **let go more often.** Allow your attention to be diverted from the accomplishment of daily tasks and the pursuit of predictable goals to the explo- ration of things, for the sake of

exploration alone. When you **break your routine** in this way, you free up creative energy that is already inside you.

Life is nothing more than a stream of experiences—the more widely and deeply you swim in it, the richer your life will be.
MIHALY CSIKSZENTMIHALYI

cultivate creativity

When I think about the word cultivate, I think garden. In order for me to have a big, orange pumpkin in October, I have to set aside some time in May to plant seeds, then I have to make sure that the growing plant gets plenty of sunlight and water, and then I have to be patient. I can't suddenly demand a pumpkin in July. It ain't gonna happen. Like pumpkins, cultivating creativity takes time. Don't rush it.

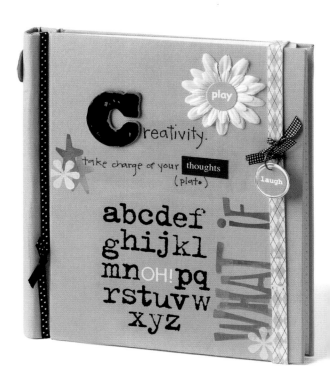

Definitely not a workbook—more than a journal, and something completely different from your sketchbook of scrapbook ideas!

With an increased awareness of your surroundings and a willingness to break away from the to-do list, you're ready for **Project Creativity**. For this, you'll need a fun book! Gather:

1. A large notebook that you can personalize

2. A place in this notebook to collect things (a page protector, a pocket or a big envelope mounted on the inside cover)

3. A closure of some kind (rubber band, clip, slip-cover—whatever you want)

This notebook will become your creativity fun book, a place to collect, record and reflect as you acknowledge creative thoughts and discover how to act on them. Creativity expert Mihaly Csikszentmihalyi suggests a daily effort to do the following:

Pay attention. Try to be surprised or amazed by something you see, hear or read about. Stop to look at an unusual car in the parking lot. Listen carefully to what a friend is saying and ask questions—don't assume you already know what she's going to say. Be open to what your world is telling you.

Avoid predictability. Try each day to surprise someone. Say something unexpected, wear a new color, or serve dessert first. Express an opinion that you haven't dared to reveal, or ask a question you wouldn't normally ask. Pick up something new at the grocery store.

Write down what you learn. This is where your fun book comes into play. Writing down how you're surprised and how you surprise others will make your experiences more concrete and enduring. After a few days, go back and read what you've recorded, and reflect on it. Don't try too hard to do something with it, just enjoy the process and revisit your entries often. At the very least, you'll begin to recognize people, places and things that encourage and inspire curiosity and creativity in you.

These simple efforts will set you off on a cool and exciting journey. I've been surprised to learn that creative thoughts (insights, unexpected ideas, solutions, connections) happen when I'm involved in easy, everyday activities. The trick is to combine an opportunity to reflect with a task that requires minimal attention (see list at lower right).

You may not have thought about these everyday activities as creative outlets before, but that's exactly what they are. It's not the environment or activity that really matters, it's the extent to which you're in harmony with it. In other words, slow the heck down and be where you are. Unplug. Turn off the radio, TV and cell phone from time to time and make a conscious effort to clear some mental space. Practice experiencing something just for the sake of experiencing it—and above all, be patient.

Not long ago, I was coloring with my youngest son and we were singing the ABC song. After several rounds, I thought about how amazing it is that 26 little letters can make a gazillion different words. I let my mind wander on to the thought that it's not

about how much material you have, because there are endless ways to combine and arrange it. Are there limitations? Nope. To remind myself of this, I used rub-on letters to put the alphabet on the front of my fun book. When I got to "M," I decided to replace the letter "o" with the expression "oh," and I laughed out loud. This is the essence of creativity— getting that "aha" or "ohhhh" insight midway through something and then acting on it. Way cool.

let it happen!

take a shower

go for a drive

walk in nature

listen to classical music

do yard work or gardening

color with children

bounce a ball or play catch

swim laps

information and inspiration

Here are a few of my favorite inspirational books and websites. They were especially helpful to me as I generated ideas for this book. Enjoy!

BOOKS

Color for Your Every Mood by *Leatrice Eisman*
Read this if you're serious about understanding the emotion behind color. I attended an amazing seminar taught by Lee, who is heralded as the international color expert.

Encyclopedia of an Ordinary Life
by *Amy Krouse Rosenthal*
In my opinion, this is a must-read for all scrapbookers. Amy and her writing style are so real. She has proven that ordinary life is interesting, important and valuable. I can't begin to tell you how buoyed up I felt about my passion for celebrating, with words and pictures, my own ordinary life. If you don't love this book, I'll buy it back from you!

Flow: The Psychology of Optimal Experience
by *Mihaly Csikszentmihalyi*
If you've ever been so engrossed in scrapbooking that you've lost all sense of time, you have experienced flow. This book is quite scientific, but very enlightening. According to the author, "People who find their lives meaningful usually have a goal that is challenging enough to take up all their energies, a goal that can give significance to their lives." Cool stuff. If nothing else, you'll feel really smart for reading it!

Creativity: Flow and The Psychology of Discovery and Invention by Mihaly Csikszentmihalyi
Same author as *Flow*. Also very scientific. I found this book fascinating because, as you might suspect, it's all about creativity—what it really is and how to get more of it into your life.

Make Your Creative Dreams Real: A Plan for Procrastinators, Perfectionists, Busy People, and People Who Would Really Rather Sleep All Day
by SARK
The author states that this book is "inner-active—that it is deliberately a little bit crooked, flawed, and intensely optimistic." For this reason, and the fact that it's just plain fun to read, I connected with this book. I think you'd enjoy it too.

The 8th Habit: From Effectiveness to Greatness
by *Stephen R. Covey*
I never made it through *The 7 Habits of Highly Effective People*, but *The 8th Habit* rocks. It's all about having vision and the amazing things that happen when you find your own unique voice and use it to help others find theirs! The principles in this book are at the heart of everything we do in scrapbooking!

You Can Do It! The Merit Badge Handbook for Grown-up Girls by *Lauren Catuzzi Grandcolas*
Lauren was one of the heroes on United Airlines Flight 93 who gave their lives to save countless others by averting the possible destruction of the U.S. Capitol or the White House. Her sisters finished this amazing book for her. I found it an incredible source of inspiration and encouragement.

WEBSITES

compendiuminc.com

Their motto is "*Live Inspired.*" I can't say enough good stuff about this company or their website. Aside from being the source for cool quote postcards (see page 88) it's a place you can go to get a lift. It's positive and affirming. Spend five minutes browsing and your head will be swimming with new ideas. If I ever quit my job at *Simple Scrapbooks*, I'm sending them my resume. They even sent me bubblegum with my order. I'm all over that.

forbetterlife.org

You've probably seen the billboards, but have you been to the site? If you love great photos and real-life stories—and I know you do—you'll come away uplifted, encouraged and ready to scrapbook.

redenvelope.com

I love the imagery of a pile of mail in which there is a red envelope—obviously a special delivery—of course you'll open it first. The Red Envelope gift catalog is brimming with cool gift ideas, many focused around photographs and memories.

russellandhazel.com

Yes! Office supply and stationary items with style. You just have to go. My creativity fun book (see page 114) is a Russell and Hazel Notebook Jacket and I love it. It's got a spring binding that will hold page protectors and the paper pad of your choice. I say splurge a little!

stranodesigns.com

If you love ribbon, you need to go here. The color combinations in their ribbon are on trend and mouth-wateringly delicious. The best news is they sell by the yard! Very cool site.

materials and design notes

chapter one | pages

4 | Simple

patterned paper (KI Memories, Lasting Impressions, Bo Bunny Press, Chatterbox) • metal-rimmed circle tags (Avery) • metal-rimmed rectangle tag (Making Memories) • ribbon (American Crafts) • stamps (Technique Tuesday) • acrylic paint • brads • silk flowers • printed ribbon

Design Notes: When you have lots of photos and you want to emphasize them equally, remove as much contrast as you can. Printing headshots of my team in black and white and presenting them in circle tags allows the reader to focus on their faces.

10 | Smitten

patterned paper (Magenta, Anna Griffin) • word accents (Making Memories) • ribbon

Design Notes: Create a strong horizontal line at "eye level" to give extra emphasis to a beautiful face! Notice how the strong green behind Trey is balanced by a small rectangle piece of green paper under the ribbon and word accents.

12 | Highlights 2004

Paper Bliss sticker (Westrim) • rub-on numbers (Chatterbox) • Bradley Hand font • ribbon • brads • jewelry tags

Design Notes: This layout is a Christmas gift, yet it highlights the events of an entire year. Don't overlook the importance of accent colors. Here, the small touches of red and green subtly communicate Christmas without causing a feeling of disharmony in this mix of multi-colored photos.

13 | Elmo

letter stickers (American Crafts) • metal-rimmed tag (Avery) • corner rounder punch (Creative Memories) • ribbon • brad • black pen

Design Notes: This page is a study in repetition. Everything about Elmo is round, so rounded photo corners, rounded sticker letters, circles and a circle tag all contribute to a harmonious outcome.

14 | Colorful You

patterned paper, Ice Candy (KI Memories) • black pen

Design Notes: Don't confuse good design with very clean, graphic pages. The playful sense of imperfection on this page works because of the order provided by the repetition of blocked photos on the left and journaling on top of a colorblocked background. Accents are placed in a visual triangle across both pages.

15 | Flowers

patterned paper (Chatterbox, Doodlebug, KI Memories) • brads (Junkitz) • silk flowers • Zig Millennium marker (EK Success) • black pen

Design Notes: When combining patterned paper, pay attention to the scale of individual patterns. The three patterns on the outside of the page are similar in scale and are a nice contrast to the smaller scale of the flower pattern around the photo.

16 | Stacy

gingham patterned paper (me and my BIG ideas) • floral patterned paper (K&Company) • rub-on letters (Making Memories) • silk flower • ribbon • brad • eyelets • string

Design Notes: Placing similar elements in opposite locations on the page will help achieve a sense of balance—here, the scripted rub-on title upper-right and the handwritten journaling tag lower-left.

17 | So Different

patterned paper, vellum (American Crafts) • rub-on letters (Making Memories) • brads

Design Notes: When you want to set up a visual comparison between photos consider a symmetrical arrangement where the photo subjects are all about the same size.

17| The Look

Arial, Gill Sans Ultra Bold condensed fonts • vellum • brads

Design Notes: I've used a consistent design scheme on every page of my *Pictures I Love* album. The colors of the journaling background and the three small squares under the title change to complement the photo. Simplifying the design in this way is an inexpensive, timesaving approach, guaranteed to be as timeless as the sentiment inside.

handwriting tote

I scrapbook standing up, but when it's time to journal, I like to find a quiet place to sit, where I can be comfortable and reflect. My handwriting tote makes it easy for me to finish scrapbook pages and cards wherever I want to—at the kitchen table, on the deck or tucked into bed, with a cup of raspberry tea. Grab a basket, bin or tote and gather together pencils, small scissors, a ruler, white eraser, scrap pieces of white cardstock and of course your favorite pens in a variety of tip sizes. Besides the portable practicality of it all, my handwriting tote just makes me happy! Learn more about the Krafter's Purse at *stonecreekcreations.com.*

18 | Mister Rogers

patterned paper (Chatterbox) • ribbon charm, metal-rimmed tag (Making Memories) • ribbon •Times Roman font

Design Notes: Pull colors from your photos. Nothing is more effective in emphasizing a single photo or focal point photo than a repetition of color. I held this photo in my hand as I scanned my pattern paper files and was delighted to find a striped pattern that combined the light blue with burgundy.

19 | Lin

patterned paper (Scrapworks) • frame (Chatterbox) • mailbox letter (Making Memories) • Comic Sans font • ribbon (May Arts)

Design Notes: I love using strips of paper. On this page, the thin white strip of paper grounds and separates the photo from the journaling. It also emphasizes the monogram "L."

20 | Home

ghost alphabet, heart (Heidi Swapp) • Monotype Corsiva font • acrylic paint

Design Notes: White space isn't space you leave white, but space on your page that you choose to leave open and free of elements. The white space on the right hand side of this page communicates a sense of spaciousness that is part of the emotion I want to convey.

21 | Homemaker

patterned paper, bookplate (KI Memories) • tailored tab (Scrapworks) • metal-rimmed tags (Making Memories) • brads

Design Notes: A hot spot of color in one of your photos (red bowl on the right) can be remedied by making it a part of a visual triangle. Notice how I added two additional red elements to incorporate it into the design—now it looks like it belongs!

22 | Why are you so good to me?

patterned paper (Making Memories, me and my BIG Ideas) • letter stickers (American Crafts) • ghost flowers, jewels (Heidi Swapp) • ribbon (Making Memories) • acrylic paint

Design Notes: If I had to assign a color to Wendy Smedley, it would be Periwinkle, a color that to me combines the constancy of blue with the creativity of purple!

23 | From Forty to 5

patterned paper (Paperfever) • chipboard number (Making Memories) • metal-rimmed tag (Avery) • safety pin (The Happy Hammer) • ribbon (Strano designs, American Crafts, Lil'Davis) • buttons • acrylic paint • stamping ink

Design Notes: This layout feels unified, because there are interesting contrasts in line and shape with a dominance of horizontal lines—in other words, contrast in line is exciting but can feel chaotic unless one type of line is used more than all the rest.

cherrios

rice krispies

corn flakes

raisin bran

frosted flakes

golden grahams

just eat some cold cereal.

BONUS IDEA!

shadow box frames

We eat a lot of cold cereal at our house, and at some point while compiling my food album (page 84) I thought, "It would be so fun to display this album in the kitchen with pictures of my boys' eating cold cereal!" You may not agree with me, but when it comes to projects like these that display photos and memories, I say "Yes, it's is a scrapbook!" You've got a stockpile of photos, why not fill your home with the evidence of your scrapbooking. Find out where you can purchase frames like these at **EKsuccess.com.**

24 | My Friend Allison

photo corners (Canson) • jewelry tag (Avery) • letter stamps (PSX) • stamping ink (Close To My Heart)

Design Notes: When placing similar photos, consider their visual strength and place them in a natural sequence. This makes the overall arrangement very easy to read.

24| Happy Boy

alphabet stamps (PSX) • photo anchor, brad (Making Memories) • CK True Type font • stamping ink (Close To My Heart)

Design Notes: Ahhh, the white space—probably the best way to give a layout an overwhelmingly clean and simple appeal.

25 | Ten

clay alphabet (Li'l Davis Designs) • black pen

Design Notes: Repetition is the key here. The colorful strips of paper in the title are repeated in the big letter "C." "C" is for Chase, and Chase is ten. Touches of white repeated on the right help achieve an easy sense of balance.

26 | Chill-dren

patterned paper, letter stickers (Pebbles, Inc.) • snowflake die cut (Ellison) • date stamp (Making Memories) • buttons • brads

Design Notes: Rather than trying to match colors exactly, try using the same "kind" of colors in your papers and other elements that are in your photos—in this case bright, playful colors work with bring playful colors. Stressing over a "perfect" match is almost always unnecessary.

27 | I Love Growing Things

patterned paper, letter stickers (Pebbles, Inc.) • buttons • brads

Design Notes: Combine detail photographs with a photograph that gives that detail some context. Visually interesting pages generally feature some contrast in photo subject.

28 | Chase, Trey & Taft

patterned paper, rub-on letters, fabric photo corner (Making Memories) • vellum pocket tag (Colorbök) • paint stripz (PM Designs) • mesh • ribbon • elastic • staples

Design Notes: When using a striped piece of patterned paper, pause to think about which direction will be better suited to the mood of your page. I initially thought a horizontal orientation would be best, repeating the strong horizontal line in the photo, but I discovered vertical stripes contributed movement and excitement that better capture our playtime in the park.

29 | School Shopping 2004

patterned paper (BasicGrey) • unbuttons (Little Black Dress Designs) • frame (Chatterbox) • letter stamps (Plaid) • stamping ink • ribbon

Design Notes: Repetition again! Round letter tiles repeat the round circles in the patterned paper and the rounded corners of the wood frame repeat the round letter tiles. Each time you add an element to your page, ask yourself if you can repeat something that is already there!

30 | Mag Mania

patterned paper (Daisy D's) • monogram letters (BasicGrey) • "mania" letters (EK Success, Making Memories) • ribbon (American Crafts) • "imagine" accent (Doodlebug) • circle accent (KI Memories) • brads (Lasting Impressions) • silk flower • staples

Design Notes: Effective collage is a balance between white space and areas of overlap. Using elements with similar color and shape will unify your design. For example, the blue rectangular "Yes!" tabs are similar in color and shape to the *Simple Scrapbooks* logo. What other similarities can you find between elements?

31 | Fly Girl

patterned paper, die cut accents (KI Memories) • letter stamps (Technique Tuesday) • ribbon • brads • staple • Bradley Hand Bold font

Design Notes: Dividing your workspace into a grid is an easy way to present a lot of information in a concise way. The left side of this layout is a 12-square grid. Each piece of memorabilia is placed in one square of the grid, and the title takes up three squares. The visual weight of the white on the right is an effective counter-balance to the left.

32 | I Love You

patterned paper (KI Memories) • rub-on letters (Making Memories) • file tab (Creative Imaginations) • gel trim (Karen Foster Design) • heart shapes (Heidi Swapp) • ribbon (Texture Trios) • eyelet • staples

Design Notes: On pages like this one, where there is a lot happening, pay attention to where you place your strongest photos. Having a clear focal point will tell the viewer where to begin. The title "I Love You" directs your eye right to the photo of Geof and I. This photo is also a part of a visual triangle with the photo of Chase and Trey (upper left) and Trey sleeping (lower right.) There are other more subtle triangles on this page and lots of repetition. Just remember, if you use it once, use it twice!

33 | He Is

patterned paper (Anna Griffin) • metal accents (K&Company) • foam stamps (Making Memories) • ribbon (Chatterbox) • acrylic paint • *song lyrics by Hilary Weeks*

Design Notes: All the elements on this page come together to create a strong feeling of harmony. The organic patterns in the paper and stamps, ornamental metal accents, satin ribbon and images subdued by vellum all feel very elegant. The individual elements "go together" and contribute to the overall formality/reverence of the message.

34 | Chase's Gift

patterned paper (Doodlebug; Pebbles, Inc.) • Designer Flair (Magic Scraps) • letter stamps (Plaid) • ribbon • stamping ink

Design Notes: The focal point of a page is sometimes where you want the eye to start and sometimes where you want it to ultimately rest. This page creates a strong clockwise flow, from the three accents up and around to the matted photo of Chase and Taft.

35 | Boys and Brothers

star stamp (Stampin' Up!) • chipboard alphabet (Heidi Swapp) • CK Fraternity font • ribbon • acrylic paint • staples

Design Notes Remember, the farther elements are placed from the midline of a two-page layout, the heavier they are in terms of visual weight. This is why the narrow strip of blue paper on the far left of this layout works to balance the large photo and title on the right. Just for fun, cover it up with your finger to see how removing it would affect the stability of the design.

36 | Favorite Fourth of July Memories

die cut accents (Pebbles, Inc.) • word plate (American Crafts) • brads (Queen and Co.) • ribbon

Design Notes: A collection of busy, everyday snapshots is simplified by using common margins in between the photos, and also by placing accents in a visual triangle.

37 | NYC

metal letters (American Crafts) • poetry dog tags (Chronicle Books) • brads • fabric • stamping ink • black pen

Design Notes: Overlapping elements in a design create a visual connection that in this case is central to the layout's message. Separated, the two elements would have carried less emotion or meaning. Handwriting the text gives it more weight, communicating the idea that the words are at least as important as the photo.

38 | Shattered Horse Dreams

chipboard letter (Li'l Davis Designs) • ribbon charm (Making Memories) • ribbon • stamping ink

Design Notes: There is a natural left to right and top to bottom flow on this page established by the horizontal lines of ribbon at the top and the title at the bottom. The resulting composition is very easy to read.

39 | Good Hair Day

fabric photo corner (Making Memories) • Zig Millennium pen (EK Success) • brad

Design Notes: A subtle visual triangle of handwriting is a counter balance to the weight of the photos on this page. Writing the main block of text vertically adds to the playfulness of the message.

40 | Treasure

Mono Mini album (Bazzill Basics) • bubble phrase (Li'l Davis Designs) • heart shape (Heidi Swapp) • Times New Roman, Papyrus fonts • ribbon

Design Notes: Keep it simple. A large image and a dominant line placed just above the midline create a pleasing proportion of image to text.

41 | Integrity Example

patterned paper (BasicGrey) • texture template window (Carolee's Creations) • cork tags, letter stickers, letter rub-ons (Creative Imaginations) • acrylic paint • CK Typewriter font • hemp • staples

Design Notes: Repetition again—regardless of the style of products used, design is strengthened by using elements twice. A small piece of the textured overlay, a cork tag and a touch of twine repeated on the right, elements introduced on the left. Notice too, the visual triangle of light tan cardstock.

42 | Clark Julian, 4th Grade

patterned paper (Keeping Memories Alive, Karen Foster Design) • letter stickers, school stickers (Karen Foster Design) • Designer Flair (Magic Scraps) • soccer ball brad (Accent Depot) • poetry dog tags (Chronicle Books) • die cut tag (Chatterbox) • sticker labels (Pebbles, Inc.) • coin envelope • library card • safety pin • brads • stamping ink

Design Notes: The formality of the left side of this layout works with the bulletin board collage because the bulletin board communicates school—it is in harmony with the subject of the page. There is a visual triangle of dot patterned paper that also acts as a visual connector.

43 | Happy Napkins

clay alphabet (Li'l Davis Designs) • ribbon • clear transparency • TwoPeas Rock Star, Times New Roman fonts • staples

Design Notes: Little touches can make a big difference! Notice how the small piece of ribbon repeated on the lower right helps maintain balance between the two sides of this layout.

44 | Every Time I Run

patterned paper (Karen Foster Design, Paper Garden) • transparency (Karen Foster Design) • shoe brads (Making Memories) • Times New Roman font • ribbon • elastic band • staples • stamping ink

Design Notes: The colors used on this layout came from the gray and gold on the road paper. Colors pulled from the photos would not have been as effective in communicating the idea of a commitment to running. There is always more than one color combination available to you—pause to think about the strength of your choice.

45 | Disco Does the Dishes

patterned paper (Lasting Impressions, O'Scrap, Mara Mi) • chipboard letters (Making Memories) • rhinestone brads (SEI) • acrylic paint

Design Notes: The combination of silver metallic paint, black polka-dot paper and rhinestones seem to shout disco! Photos aside, the elements you use can clearly establish a particular theme. When they do, and this theme supports your photos, the result is harmony.

46 | Unlucky

alphabet stamps (Technique Tuesday) • metal-rimmed tag (Avery) • CK Typewriter font • ribbon • acrylic paint • black pen

Design Notes: The concept of this page obviously began with an idea, not a photo and is more about the list of "unlucky" items than anything else. Giving the journaling lots of room and varying the handwriting style gives it the weight it deserves. The random placement of individual list items allows me to add more items as I encounter them!

47 | Halloween 2003

patterned paper, Ice Candy (KI Memories) • chipboard letter (Li'l Davis Designs)• black pen

Design Notes: There are three visual triangles at work on this layout: one of rounded rectangular shapes, one of dimensional elements and one of photos. Incorporating visual triangles in your design is one of the easiest ways to establish a sense of balance across two pages.

48 | The Persistence of Yellow

paint stripz (PM designs) • alphabet stamps (Hero Arts) • tag (Westrim Crafts) • Inspirables stone (EK Success) • ribbon (Close to My Heart) • silk flowers • stamping ink

Design Notes: The horizontal line continuing out from tag title is a strong visual connector on this page that helps move the eye along from left to right. Repeating the stamped "yellow" from the title on the journaling page also has a unifying affect.

49 | Studio Time

chipboard letters (Heidi Swapp) • American Typewriter font • jewelry tag • ribbon • brad • acrylic paint

Design Notes: Repeating the contrasting combination of white, green and black from the title on the lower right of this spread is very unifying. The black-and-white clock photo is also an exciting contrast against the other colorful photos.

50 | Why I Still Believe

patterned paper (Anna Griffin, Flair Designs) • chipboard words (Li'l Davis Designs) • ribbon bow (Anna Griffin) • tags (Avery) • metal charm (Making Memories) • American Typewriter font • flower charm • brad • stamping ink • ribbon

Design Notes: Everything on this page contributes to a feel of nostalgia. Even the techniques of paper tearing, stitching and aging add to the homespun appeal. Also, take advantage as often as you can of the expertise that goes into the design of coordinating product lines. All four of the base papers on this page are from the same Christmas line.

51 | Left

chipboard letters (Li'l Davis Designs) • CK True Type font

Design Notes: The wordplay of "Left" on this page is an underused application of repetition. It's subtle, but very effective.

52 | Ode to Chocolate

leather bookplate, corner (Making Memories) • ribbon (Strano Designs) • brads (Karen Foster Design) • Zig Millennium pen (EK Success)

Design Notes: Nothing emphasizes a message like a telling photo made really big. Notice how the pink and brown introduced in the ribbon is repeated with pink brads and brown leather accents.

53 | Clark's Dynamite Birthday

number die cuts (QuicKutz) • notebook paper • masking tape • staples • black pen

Design Notes: A confident designer works in styles that please the intended audience. My almost teenage son doesn't want "cute," or whatever new look appeals to me. He deserves a birthday layout that will reflect his current tastes and interests. Notice how the simple addition of an arrow and a number "12" complete a visual triangle of yellow.

54 | I Am Their Demographic

Coluzzle circle die cuts (Provo Craft) • brads • staples

Design Notes: The visual triangle of colorful elements on the right side of this layout work to counterbalance it against the collage of photos and memorabilia on the left.

55 | Boston

Jolee's stickers (EK Success) • letter stamps (Technique Tuesday) • quote stamp (Hero Arts) • stamping ink

Design Notes: The top and bottom borders of vellum over photos combine with the orange paper strips as an easy structure for the other photos. Isolating the photo of Chase above the midline communicates quickly that this layout is about Chase in Boston.

56 | All This

concho (Scrapworks) • brads (Junkitz) • corner rounder punch (Creative Memories) Times Roman font • black pens

Design Notes: The combination of paper strips and rounded corners repeated on both sides of this layout simplifies and unifies the design of this page.

57 | Stone Soup

letter stickers (Bo Bunny Press) • brads (Making Memories)

Design Notes: The green background on this page is placed so that it emphasizes Taft over the other children—he is of course the most important child pictured here! Thin white journaling strips on the right are a repetition of the journaling on the left.

58 | Scooter

metal frames (Making Memories) • letter stickers, brads (American Crafts) • Trimz (Junkitz) • metal-rimmed tag (Avery) • Century Gothic font • number stamps (PSX) • stamping ink

Design Notes: The visual triangle of green metal frames and white used opposite itself establish balance across these two pages.

59 | Oregon Coast

transparency lay-over (My Mind's Eye) • metal charm (Making Memories) • ribbon (American Crafts) • square punch (Marvy Uchida) • mesh • number brads • staples

Design Notes: A 20-square grid on the right showcases a combination of photos that visually describe our ocean trip. Using mesh and ribbon on both sides of the layout and incorporating a square title are examples of the repetition that unifies the design.

60 | The Lambsons

patterned paper (Memory Box) • label (Junkitz) • chipboard letter, decorative tape (Heidi Swapp) • brads (SEI) • ribbon (American Crafts) • date stamp • letter stamps (PSX) • stamping ink • black pen

Design Notes: The colors in the fabric label accent are repeated in the paper strips on the top right of this spread, and a visual triangle is introduced by the placing an additional strip of light blue under one of the date stamps, bottom right. These little touches go a long way in achieving a sense of stability or balance.

61 | Every Nook and Cranny

patterned paper (EK Success; Rusty Pickle; Pebbles, Inc.) • letter stickers (EK Success) • stickers (K&Company) • letter stamps (Plaid) • tag clips (Karen Foster Design) • buttons • brads • stamping ink

Design Notes: A six-photo grid and the repetition of the gingham paper and buttons on the bottom right give this collage-style page a sense of order.

chapter two | projects

64-66 | Mom According To...

preservation album, monogram coasters, letter stickers, rub-ons (SEI) • patterned paper (SEI, Making Memories, Daisy D's) • printed vellum (Stampin' Up!) • flower buttons (Doodlebug Design) • photo corners (Heidi Swapp) • brads • ribbon • chalk • jewelry tags • *title page photo by Amy Raab*

Design Notes: The design of this album is totally inspired by SEI's coordinated line, Aunt Gertie's Garden—the album is for me, and so are the colors! The interview format is an easier read in an horizontal orientation. Don't hesitate turning your album on it's side if it feels better that way!

67 | Trey Speaks

patterned paper, jewelry tags, small brads (Doodlebug Design) • tags (Avery) • large brads (SEI) • ribbon

Design Notes: I love how the square photos and square patterned paper is repetitious of the square accordion album pages. Black-and-white photos and black journaling play really well off each other.

68-69 | Close to My Heart

patterned paper (Close to My Heart) • stamps (Close to My Heart, Making Memories) • tags (avery) • ribbon • brads • stamping ink

Date Nights

patterned paper (SEI) • ribbon • letter stamps (Precision Art Stamps) • stamping ink • metal-rimmed tag • staples • tags

Design Notes: Coordinated papers are perfectly suited to mini-albums like these. For best results limit the number of patterns you use to three or four, and vary the scale and type of pattern for visual interest—in other words, don't use two stripes when you could use a stripe and a polka dot or a stripe and a swirl pattern.

70-75 | Where in Spokane

9 x 9 album, rub-ons (Making Memories) • patterned paper, vellum (American Crafts) • photo corners (Canson) • Comic Sans font • ribbon

Design Notes: When you are compiling a theme album with sections, consider using a line of coordinating product that features several colors. This will allow you to use color to help distinguish sections from each other. Use a little of your chosen color on every page of that section.

76-77 | Family Labels

6 x 6 album (Provo Craft) • patterned paper (Flair Design; Patchwork Paper Design, Inc.; Scenic Route; Sweetwater) • labelz, photo turnz (Junkitz), book binding tape, label holders (Making Memories) • CK Leisurely font • brads • ribbon • acrylic paint • Xyron adhesive

Design Notes: To save time, I often use the same design scheme on pages of theme albums. The colors and patterns may change, but the arrangement of elements is consistent, and easy to assemble. This consistency also becomes a unifying element for the page-to-page flow of the album.

78-81 | Grandma Addie

2-minute Memories Scrapbook Card (Simple Scrapbooks) • patterned paper (Daisy D's) • woven letter (Making Memories) • rub-ons (Chatterbox) • ribbon • buttons • brad • silk flower • stamping ink

Design Notes: A monochromatic color scheme makes the work of designing small projects that feature a variety of colorful photographs very easy. Just pick a color that communicates the message or captures the personality of your subject and stay within that color family. More good news: limiting your color palette in this way will make your mini-album easier to view too!

82-83 | Remember the Magic Album

7 x 7 album (Creative Memories) • patterned paper (Pebbles, Inc.; Lasting Impressions) • Disney die-cuts (Paper Garden) • small Mickey die cut (SandyLion) • dimensional Mickey sticker (EK Success) • rub-ons, tags (Making Memories) • slide mount • ribbon • brads • Comic Sans font

Design Notes: This album is example of creating a design scheme for an entire section. In this case, each section is made up of three, two-page spreads. Once you have one section designed, the others come together very quickly, as you simply drop photos and elements into place!

84-85 | The Food We Will Remember

8 x 8 album (Pioneer) • large letter stamps (Technique Tuesday) • small letter stamps (Plaid) • large metal-rimmed tags (Making Memories) • small metal rimmed tags (EK Success) • ribbon (Scrapbook Wizard) • brads • acrylic paint

Design Notes: The four colors that make up the color scheme for this album were inspired in part by the fact that they are often used in food packaging. I knew that these colors would work together and work with all the bits and pieces I intended to use. Using color consistently in a collage-style design really helps the readability. Most pages in this album are very busy, these are broken up by a handful of pages laid out in a four-square grid. These more structured pages act as a relative rest for the eye when you view page after page.

86-87 | Marathon album

6 x 6 album (O'Scrap) • wooden numbers (Michaels) • patterned paper (Doodlebug Designs, Bo Bunny Press, American Crafts) • letter stamps (Plaid) • vellum envelope (Colorbök) • flower buttons, tokens (Doodlebug Designs) • metal-rimmed tags (Making Memories) • acrylic paint • Staz-On stamping ink (Tsukinecko) • brads • ribbon • bobby pins

Design Notes: Monochromatic color schemes make assembling little albums like this so easy! Just cut up a variety of patterned papers and put them in a pile, next to your photos and start slapping stuff together. I of course had my green color drawer next to me with all kinds of accent choices—so easy!

88 | Compendium Post Cards

postcards (Compendium, Inc.) • metal star (Making Memories) • alphabet stamp (PSX) • jump ring • ribbon • brad • stamping ink

Design Notes: Not much designing here, just a matter of pairing a photo with the words of a quote. Staz-On ink let me add my own words to the surface of each photo which definitely adds visual interest!

89 | It's All About Me!

2⅛ x 4 tin (Target) • patterned paper (KI Memories, Making Memories, Scenic Route) • vellum envelope (EK Success) • metal flower, metal-rimmed tag (Making Memories) • letter tab (Scrapworks) • Ice Candy (KI Memories) • small metal flowers (The Happy Hammer) • photo corners (Canson) • jewelry tags (Avery) • small brads (The Happy Hammer) • large brads (American Crafts) • ribbon (Textured Trios) • stamping ink

Design Notes: Here again, it's all about color. I love starting with an album or container that inspires a fun color scheme. I store my patterned papers in big files by color, so all I had to do was hold my little tin in one hand while I thumbed through my paper files—the appropriate patterns just seemed to jump out at me when I do this.

90-95 | May, Everyday Album

6 x 12 album (Westrim) • patterned paper (me and my BIG ideas) • foam letter stamps (Lil'Davis Designs) • number stamps (PSX) • metal accent (KI Memories) • silk flowers • ribbon • brads • acrylic paint • stamping ink

Design Notes: The design scheme for this album was really determined my the combination of page protectors, but it nonetheless works with the ribbon inspired color scheme to contribute a strong sense of unity to an album that features a huge variety of photos and memorabilia!

96-97 | Girls Weekend

canvas bags (Innovo, inc.) • patterned paper (from Stacy's scrap bin) • brads (Making Memories) • stamps (Hero Arts) • buttons • ribbon • silk flowers

Design Notes: The use of small scale patterns and light bright colors kept this entire project looking coordinated. One of the best things you can do to save time and create harmony in a multi-piece project like this is to limit the product you use!

98-99 | Without a Doubt

6 x 6 album (Pulp Paper Products) • patterned paper (Scrapworks) • flowers (Doodlebug) • fabric pocket (Hot Off the Press) • altered quote book (Compendium, Inc.) • acrylic flower (KI Memories) • Times New Roman font • brads • ribbon

Design Notes: This is another album-inspired color scheme. Since there are no photos inside the album, the best design tip is related to type. I like traditional, serif

fonts that won't be hard to read. Actually, the best design tip is this: Always be willing to learn, but also be willing to ask for help in areas that you find challenging. Don Lambson helped me format my journaling in this album. Thanks, Don!

chapter three | other stuff

106-111 | Stacy's Albums

Family Fun Library—these albums are no longer available. I'm so sorry. Believe me, I wish they were!

School of Life, Kindergarten—patterned paper (Rusty Pickle, K&Company, O'Scrap, Hot off the Press) • designer flair (Magic Scraps) • chipboard letter (Making Memories) • photo turns, brads (Junkitz) • stamping ink

School of Life–Title—patterned paper (Creative Imaginations) • stickers (Pebbles, Inc.) • tailored letters, tabs (Scrapworks) • measuring tape • buttons • staples

Family Celebrations—12 x 12 album (Making Memories)

Just Because—12 x 12 album (Making Memories) • Berlin Sans FB font

Photos I Love—8 x 8 album (We R Memory Keepers) • alphabet stamps (PSX) • stamping ink

Sing-Along—8½ x 11 album (Frances Meyer, Inc.) • bookplate (Making Memories) • brads (Karen Foster Design) • Berlin Sans FB font

miscellaneous

Notes from Stacy

black pens (American Crafts, EK Success and Sakura) • chalk pencils (The General Pencil Company)

102 | Love (Shadow Box)

picture shadow box (Michaels) • patterned paper (KI Memories) • foam letter stamps, metal-rimmed tag, metal flower, brads (Making Memories) • letter stamps (PSX) • printed ribbon (Lavish Lines) • ribbon (Textured Trios) • acrylic paint

102 | Clark and Chase Frames

frames (Michaels) • alphabet stamps (Plaid) • metal-rimmed tag (Avery) • ribbon • stamping ink • acrylic paint

stacy's tags

I love these tags! They're a work in progress. And I'm enjoying the chance to gather together, from so many sources, ideas that will enrich my scrapbook story.

I'm using both sides of each tag, and sometimes even tracing a tag to make a second, if I need more room. Even the effort to describe my scrapbooking style, list personal sources of inspiration, or gather together happy colors has helped me recognize and celebrate what's unique about me.

I plan to hang my tag book on a peg in my studio, and use it as an inspiration piece to help me capture the extraordinary and everyday memories that are me. My hope is that it will challenge me to step back often and remember the big picture behind my scrapbooking hobby.

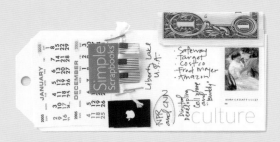

culture — Liberty Lake U.S.A. · Safeway · Target · Costco · Fred Meyer · Amazon · NPR and CNN

music — Eine kleine Nacht Musik ♥ · when i listen: Sunday a.m. · on my jogs · in the car · cleaning house · on airplanes

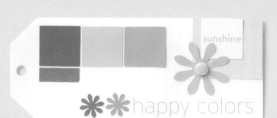

spirituality

rituals

sunshine · **happy colors**

· everyday photos · handwriting · lots of color · random stories · pleasing imperfection · I absolutely love... stripes and ginghams · mini-brads · abc stamps · cardstock in all colors · ❀ what is your *style*?

□ cute □ clean □ collage □ shabby □ classic

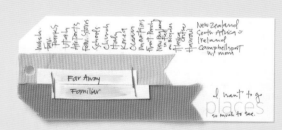

Far Away / Familiar · *places* · New Zealand · South Africa · Utah · Ireland · New England · Alaska · Hawaii · Campbell Sport w/ mom · I want to go so much to see.

friends · I'm so lucky! · College · Idaho Joanne JaNiese · Chicago Penny Julie

defining moments

← Extended Family

※ Favorite Dishes · Danish salad · corn casserole · Italian chicken · pasta fagioli · hash brown potatoes · fruit pies, cobblers · creamy soups · salads w/ lots of stuff · sandwiches w/ milk · *delicious*

my marriage · my testimony · great kids · exercise · comfortable home · work w/ sibling · value simple moments · creativity.

Goals and *accomplishments* · hard work and lots of luck.

final thoughts

Buying silk flowers in bulk is **always** a good idea.

Any time you pair a memory with a photo, you are scrapbooking. (This means scrapbooks come in all shapes and sizes and can even be hung on the wall!)

There are times when you don't need your camera. **Leave** it at home.

Staz-On ink is just about the coolest thing ever—buy some.

You should embrace your handwriting—at least some of the time.

Both events and moments pages are really about the people experiencing them. **Scrapbook people**.

Making Memories rub-ons deserve best product-design of the century award. Talk about form follows function!

Learning to evaluate pages for proven principles of design is the **best thing** you can do to train your inner designer.

One can **never have too many** mini-brads. (I used 138 in this book!)

Black gingham and polka-dot ribbon goes with everything! Need proof? Re-read this book!

The **story** you are most qualified to tell is your own. If you don't do it, who will?

Alphabet stamps are a great investment. Purchase as many sets as you wish—no excuses or justification needed here.

I think Gloo is **my new favorite** dimensional adhesive!

I think my children will ask to see pictures of themselves, and the people and places they love. I think it won't matter if those pictures are in date order.

I think that there is **much more to this hobby** than pictures, pretty papers and finished pages or projects.

I think scrapbooking is a way to **live with passion**. It's about being present in your life. It's about recognizing a fleeting moment as **memorable** before it passes and it's about the ability you have to say, "**I was here**, I lived and breathed and played in the sand. I learned and I loved. **I laughed and I cried** and I danced to disco in my kitchen."

i think there's a **big** picture.
what about you?